GW00776398

The World of
Fred Spalding

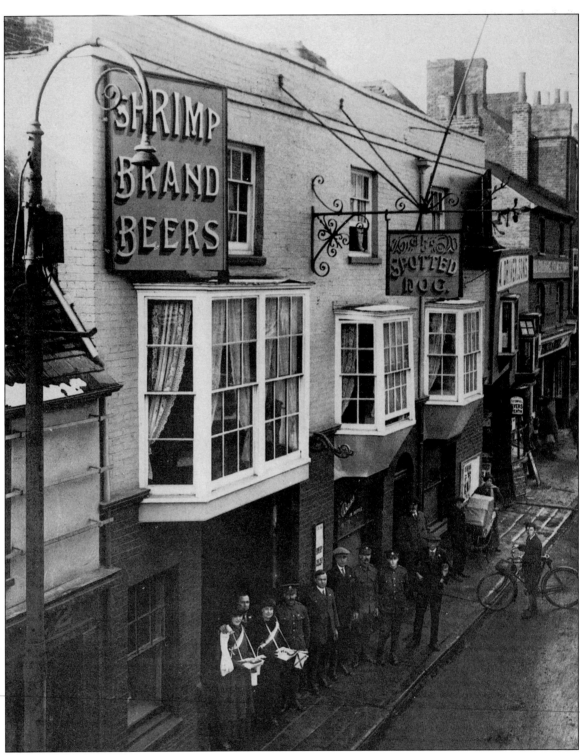

The Spotted Dog in Tindal Street, Chelmsford: one of the now vanished landmarks recorded by the camera of Fred Spalding

The World of Fred Spalding

PHOTOGRAPHS OF ESSEX

1860–1940

Introduced by
Stan Jarvis

1992

Contents

Published by the
ESSEX RECORD OFFICE
County Hall, Chelmsford CM1 1LX

© ESSEX COUNTY COUNCIL

All rights reserved
This book may not be reproduced in whole or in part,
in any form, without written permission from the publishers.

British Library Cataloguing-in-Publication Data
A catalogue record of this book is available from the British Library.

ISBN 0 900360 93 3

Essex Record Office Publication No. 121

Designed by Keith Mirams MCSD
Printed in England by Lavenham Press Limited

Preface

THE SPALDING PHOTOGRAPHIC ARCHIVE – some 7000 images, created by three generations of Spaldings – has been for nearly 40 years one of the treasures of the Essex Record Office. At an average of less than two photographs per week over the life of the firm, it can only be a fraction of what once existed, and even the survivors cluster thickly towards the firm's later years. Yet the collection remains unrivalled for its depiction of the changes and continuities of late nineteenth and early twentieth-century Essex.

The archive's true value was long concealed by the fact that perhaps four out of every five images do not survive as prints, but only as fragile glass plates, measuring up to 12 by 10 inches. Some plates have original labels, or a place-name scratched into the emulsion; others carry no identifying marks at all, and none of the firm's work records now survive. In 1986, however, the Record Office completed a programme of copying and printing the plates, and a selection was shown in a highly successful exhibition.

Demand for a publication based on the Spaldings' work was already obvious. Here – finally – is a further selection of photographs, introduced by Stan Jarvis, a leading writer on old Essex. The images themselves have been chosen, and captions written, by Chris Lambert, one of the archivists at the Record Office. The glass plates were originally copied and researched by the members of a Manpower Services Commission training project, and we are also grateful to those many members of the public who have contributed their knowledge of particular scenes.

Fred Spalding, head of the firm from the 1880s onwards, was primarily a working photographer, not an artist or an historian. With the loss of nearly all his portrait work, it is hard now to judge how well he caught a likeness, but he certainly took aesthetic considerations into account in the landscapes and townscapes which he meant to publish as postcards. And he became increasingly fascinated by the history of his neighbourhood and the changes it was undergoing. But there are still many photographs which merely record what the client wished to have recorded: a building under construction; a new crop-sprayer; a shop front that could be reproduced in advertisements. We have chosen what seem to us the most evocative, informative and surprising, but all users of the collection will have their own favourites.

The value of such visual archives is increasingly recognized by users and archivists alike. The vulnerability of photographs to physical damage and chemical decay, and the ease with which information about their history and subjects can be lost, makes it vital to treat them well: to record their contents, to keep them under controlled conditions, and to copy them as a safeguard against loss. Even on the Spalding collection, work remains to be done, but we hope that this book will help further to spread awareness of our pictorial heritage, and so help to preserve it.

The World of Fred Spalding

FREDERICK SPALDING THE ELDER, founding father, as we might call him, of the photographer's art in Chelmsford, was born in Danbury in about 1810. His early life is totally obscure, but in the 1850s he went into business in the county town. An interesting man, he had more than one line. The directory of Essex for 1859 shows him under 'Naturalists' and describes him as a 'bird stuffer and furniture broker'. He kept up with the latest ideas, though, and saw photography as the new art. Within two years he had mastered the complex, bulky equipment and the chemical processes. The 1861 census records him as a 'photographer etc.', and by 1862 the directory has altered its entry to 'picture-frame maker and photographer, Duke Street'. He also appears under the heading 'Photographic Artists' as the only one practising in Chelmsford, and in that very year he photographed the Chelmsford Charity School boys in their uniform, very much under the watchful eye of their master, Joseph Mitchell (*see page 70*).

This was obviously the way forward. 'Bird-stuffing' was discontinued. Photography caught on, albeit still a rich man's indulgence. The 1866 directory shows Frederick Spalding established as 'photographer and fancy repository', in premises in Tindal Square.

The Frederick who followed so successfully in his footsteps – the eldest of his nine children and hero of our story – was born in Duke Street of his first wife, Eliza, and baptised in Chelmsford cathedral (then simply the parish church) on 3 July 1858. His father was shown as a 'trunk-maker'.

Fred grew up, under his father's influence, in the fascinating world of photography. At seven years old he posed for a portrait in his father's studio, kneeling on a chair, with one arm propped on an album of his father's work and the other hand negligently placed in a pocket –

all cleverly arranged to make the boy keep as still as possible while the plate was exposed in the camera.

The system which his father had taught himself was the wet collodion method, invented by Frederick Scott Archer in 1851. A glass plate was coated with a mixture of collodion (gun cotton dissolved in ether) and potassium iodide, sensitized with a solution of silver nitrate, and then exposed for anything between 2 seconds and $1^1/_2$ minutes, developed and fixed – while still damp – to produce a glass negative. Only in the 1880s were these 'wet' plates replaced by faster 'dry' plates using gelatin.

In the days of collodion, prints were usually made on albumen paper, coated with egg-white. Modern-type gelatin silver prints were introduced from the 1880s onwards, but the Spaldings followed other Victorian photographers in

The young Frederick, photographed in his father's studio in Tindal Square. Fred's birth in 1858 dates this image to the mid-1860s, but it also shows stylistic features typical of the early years of studio photography. The combination of chair, book and full-length portrait is rarely found after the 1860s, and the elaborately childish clothes of the later 1800s have yet to emerge. Only a little later, and Fred would have been at distinct risk of a sailor suit.

'All the world is a-wheel. All classes and all ages have come under the domination of the bicycle.' Thus the 'Essex Weekly News' in 1899 on one of the great crazes of the previous 30 years, in which Fred Spalding played a full part. Here he is in an over-painted photograph, posed heroically with one of the huge front-pedal drive machines of about 1880, and wearing the uniform of the West Essex Bicycling Club, formed in 1875.

trying a wide variety of printing processes, including the carbon print and the platinotype, in the search for a photograph that would not fade.

To accommodate his well-off patrons and to get as much natural light on the subject as possible, our Fred's father built a studio of glass and corrugated iron on top of the house and shop in Tindal Square. Though painted over, it can still be seen up there today.

Young Fred grew up in the house above the shop, and went to the Grammar School – still then in Duke Street – along with other tradesmen's sons. He had a sense of fun, an enjoyment of life which was still evident in 1930 when he described to a Y.M.C.A. audience some of those happy childhood days of 60 years before.

The short journey to school, for example, was achieved with a little teasing of 'Dilly Miller'. The Victorians called anybody who was a little simple-minded, 'dilatory' – the boys, of course, shortened it. On market days Dilly had to thread a rope through a row of posts with holes in the top, ranging down the street, to keep cattle out of the shops. The rope was also used by farmers for hitching their horses – forerunner of the multi-storey car park!

The boys would lie in wait until Dilly was on his way, carefully threading the rope – then they would dart out, Fred included, and tie a knot which would not go through the hole in the post and so stopped the poor old fellow in his tracks.

In young Fred's day the gravelled High Street still had a stream of water running down it from the site of the conduit in Tindal Square. The same Dilly Miller was employed to dam this stream with sacking, forming a pool from which he splashed the water all across the road to lay the dust, using a wooden shovel very deftly. Fred and company knew he loved to talk about fishing. They held him in conversation while one of their number slipped down to the pool, pulled aside the sacking and ran off, leaving Dilly to start all over again. 'My mother,' said Fred, 'has often made me buy some shag tobacco to give the old gentleman, perhaps to condone my misdeeds!'

From his own accounts the young Fred was just the type of boy to enjoy the fairs which were then such a feature in Chelmsford's calendar. For two days in both May and November the fun of the fair took over the very High Street, running half way down from Tindal Square. The square itself was crowded with the fair people's caravans and with booths selling all sorts of goodies and knick-knacks. Fred recalls:

'I have seen as many as four roundabouts in the streets – three in Tindal Square and one in front of the cannon. There were shows of every description – cheap jacks, strong men, fat women, peep shows, clowns, jugglers, shooting galleries, in fact, all the fun of the fair . . . It was interesting in the early morning to see these fair people before they commenced business – living in their caravans, washing the children, cooking their breakfast, making the fair rock and many other things.'

The fair in November was almost outshone by the doings on Guy Fawkes day. Fred tells us: 'I have seen many lively times. On one occasion the bonfire (on the Fairfield, off Duke Street) burnt out before the usual time, so some of those

F. SPALDING,
PHOTOGRAPHER,
Fancy Repository and General Toy Warehouse,
CONDUIT-SQUARE, CHELMSFORD.

ALBUMS, WORK BOXES, AND WRITING DESKS.
LADIES' TRAVELLING CASES, RETICULES, &c.
PORTMANTEAUS, TRUNKS, AND BOXES.
VASES, LUSTRES, &c.
CROQUET AND ARCHERY.
CHRISTMAS PRESENTS IN GREAT VARIETY.
REVOLVING STEREOSCOPE, with Slides,
And MAGIC LANTERNS, on Hire.

The 'Essex Almanac' in 1865 carried the first advertisement yet traced for the Spalding firm. Photography tops the bill, but is still one novelty amongst others.

Spalding, a prominent tradesman, a member of the Borough Council for 54 years, and mayor for 3, was proud of his town – and also of the displays with which he filled his long High Street frontage of plate glass. However, the wide variety of the shop's goods and his own enthusiasms could produce surprising combinations. On the left is Fred in his robes as Mayor of Chelmsford (1922–4), from a photograph in the collection of the Chelmsford and Essex Museum. On the right are demonstrations of his local patriotism in the borough arms of 1889, and of his photographic skills, but the handbags strike a rather jarring note.

Crowds await the arrival of Father Christmas outside Spalding's High Street shop. The presence of the Tindal Café (always advertised as 'over Mr. Spaldings') dates this picture to 1927 or later.

PHOTOGRAPHIC STUDIO,
TOY & FANCY BAZAAR,
3, Tindal St. CHELMSFORD.

F. SPALDING,
PORTRAIT & LANDSCAPE PHOTOGRAPHER,

*Is now working a new and instantaneous process in Photography,
specially adapted for Children, Groups and Animals.*

All kinds of Pictures carefully copied, enlarged, or
reduced, painted in oil or water colours, prices and sizes
on application.—See the Permanent Carbon Enlargement.

The REV. W. R. PARKER, Willingale Spain Rectory, writes—

" I wish to express to you the great satisfaction the enlarged
Photo. of my mother gives me and my sister also. We really marvel
that a likeness so true should have been effected from the one sent to
you ; moreover, their is a delicacy and softness in the work that we
both appreciate. The framing, too, we think is in excellent taste."

*(This was done from a very old Photo., and is only one of numerous unsolicited
Testimonials.)*

Framing & Re-gilding Oak & Gold Frames of every Description.

Large and varied Assortment of Useful and Fancy Goods suitable for
Wedding and other Presents.

*F. S. has always on hand a large and varied stock of Portmanteaus,
Bags, Dress Trunks, Purses, Tin, Wood, and other Boxes, Lawn Tennis,
Croquet, Albums, Work Boxes, Baskets, Desks, Inkstands, and other
Goods, to numerous to Catalogue.*

Any particulars, Lists of Prices, & any Article not in Stock
procured or made on Application.
AN INSPECTION RESPECTFULLY SOLICITED.

ALL KINDS OF GAMES AND AMUSEMENTS ON SALE CR LET ON HIRE.

F. S. can supply a good and select ENTERTAINMENT of DIS-
SOLVING VIEWS for Private Parties, Schools, &c., by either Oil or
Lime Light (see Opinions of Press and Private Testimonials). Fresh
Subjects, &c., every Year.

*Spalding's advertisement in the 'Chelmsford Directory' of 1881
makes it clear that photography is now the leading element in the
business. The 'new and instantaneous process' is probably the dry
gelatin plate, which at this time was replacing the slower wet
collodion.*
Reproduced by courtesy of Chelmsford Library

present began to help themselves to gates and
other inflammable materials from the surround-
ing premises. One man brought a bundle of faggot wood. A well-known resident saw him and
said, 'That's right, boys, bring them along' – and
they did.

'The next morning the same gentleman found
his stack of faggot wood gone. He little thought
it was his own property he had told them to
burn. The 5th of November celebrations became
very rowdy during the next few years and were
stopped by the police, with the assistance of
special constables, my father being one of these.'

Fred grew up watching his father making his
magical pictures – a portrait artist in chemicals
– and had a go himself. Of all nine children he
was the one to follow in his father's footsteps.

In the 1870s he was understudying his father
in the business of portrait photography and in
the running of the shop. Was it his idea or his
father's to take pictures of places? I like to think

it was the young man's enthusiasm and energy,
as well as the development of the art itself which
started 'Spalding's' on the road leading in the
1890s to picture postcards.

With young Fred's increasing competence in
photography and in the shop selling basketry
and fancy goods of all kinds, his father was able
to retire to Lathcoats Farm at Galleywood,
which he had longed to do, and to settle down
to the popular pastime, apparently still practised
today, of making a loss at farming.

I am sure this must have been before 1881,
because the 'Chelmsford Directory' of that date
came out with a full-page advertisement for
'Spalding's' – an unusual step which may indicate that our Fred was telling the world that his
business was now on a new footing and ready to
boom, with all the confidence and éclat of the
independent young businessman.

In 1888, when he was 30, Fred Spalding was
visited by the British Industrial Publishing Company, publishers of a projected 'historical, statis-
tical and biographical' account of the eastern
counties. They clearly hoped to get sufficient
payment from the businesses represented to
make a profit on the enterprise. Naturally, when
the publication appeared in 1890 it was written
in what might be called a congratulatory tone.
Since it outlines so clearly Fred's circumstances
at that time, we set out the extract covering his
business:

'F. Spalding, Portrait and Landscape Photographer, 3 Tindal Square (opposite Corn
Exchange) – What used in the benighted days of
wet plates to be called the 'Black Art' has an able
representative in Chelmsford in the person of
Mr. Frederick Spalding, Portrait and Landscape
Photographer, whose studio is situated opposite
the Corn Exchange. In addition, however, to the
photographic business, Mr. Spalding has also a
flourishing trade in fancy goods, bags, and useful articles, etc..

'The premises (*see page 22*) . . . are of three sto-
ries in height, and have two capital windows, in
one of which there is a fine array of photographs, while the other is devoted to the other
goods mentioned, of which the shop, which is
spacious and well appointed, has a large stock
of all the latest novelties on view. On the first
floor are rooms for framing and regilding, also a
reception or waiting-room, and a dressing-room
for the convenience of ladies. The studio . . . is at
the top of the house, is well arranged, and has
all the most recent appliances for regulating the
lighting of sitters, etc.. Here a variety of cameras
and other apparatus and accessories is at hand
for the production of negatives of all sizes, while

all facilities are also at hand for enlarging, reproducing, etc., etc..

'Portraiture and landscape photography are the principal, but by no means the only branches for Mr. Spalding also undertakes the photographing of mansions, interiors, fat stock, horses, groups, machinery, etc., either as photographs or for reproduction by the many printing processes with which photography is now so closely allied. Mr. Spalding makes a speciality of enlargements, and has recently executed orders of H.R.H. the Prince of Wales for photographs of one of His Royal Highness's horses named 'Sun of York', which was prize winner at the Essex Agricultural Show, and was photographed by Mr. Spalding, and enlarged to 23 x 17. On receipt of the first copy His Royal Highness sent an order for three more the same size, besides smaller ones. At the time of our visit we noticed two very fine enlargements of Mr. Edward Corder, Alderman Essex C. C., and Chairman of the Chelmsford Board of Guardians. One of these, a vignetted head by the carbon process, is to be presented to Mr. Corder by his brother Guardians, and the other, which is painted in oils, is to be hung in the Board Room of the new Union House; both portraits are striking likenesses, and the finish excellent. We also saw enlargements from negatives taken by Mr. Spalding at Easton Lodge (by an order from Lady Brooke) on the occasion of the Prince of Wales' visit. The group contains capital portraits of His Royal Highness, Lord and Lady Brooke, Lord Randolph Churchill, Sir Henry Selwin and Lady Ibbetson, Count Deym, the Hereditary Prince of Hohenlohe, etc., etc..

'Mr. Spalding personally superintends each department of his establishment, and from other specimens of his art which we had the pleasure of inspecting – especially some reproductions from old faded photos, the results to us seemed almost impossible looking at the sources from which they were obtained. We also noticed a number of photographs of the county gentry, their mansions, the churches, and other places of interest in and around Chelmsford. We feel sure that every care and attention is given to orders entrusted to him, and his establishment will at any time well repay a visit.'

That the Corn Exchange should be mentioned as a guide to his address is apposite, for Fred became well-known as an entrepreneur, bringing all sorts of shows to the Corn Exchange, dashing across from the shop to make last minute arrangements. And he was ready to drop everything to get that essential photograph. A classic example is the record he made of the Great Flood of August 1888 (*see page 33*), photographing the swollen river and its invasion of the town from every stand-point.

In his private life, too, Fred had been active. He courted Emma Agnes Darby and they were married in 1885. As far as I can trace, there was nobody there to take a wedding photograph! In the early 1890s, now living himself in the Broomfield Road, he moved his shop and studio to 4 High Street, with rooms also at the end of Crane Court, and shortly afterwards the Tindal Square premises were given up. One son was born in 1890, and he was called Frederick – to take the business on in the same name for three generations.

Now a settled family man, with his business on a sound footing, Fred felt able to employ staff and take more commissions for location photography. From his shop he travelled about indefatigably, building up an enormous collection of views to be reproduced as postcards for sale in his gift shop. In producing these, Spalding added his individual, rather endearing touches. Where he felt the sky was too intrusive over a broad view of Essex marshland, he would add a few – or many – birds in flight, carefully drawn in on a print, which would then be re-photographed for the finished effect. Later he even drew in an aeroplane to add interest to a wedding group.

Village streets in the days before the motor car looked wide and empty, especially as foregrounds to popular postcards. Spalding solved the problem by positioning willing village lads all down the street, and photographing them in an eternal game of leap-frog! This ploy is almost Spalding's trade mark in numerous Essex village scenes. But this was a harmless enough practice and Spalding made a wonderful job of the finished photograph. He could command a pose from the Prince of Wales in distinguished company at the Earl of Warwick's place at Little Easton (*see page 51*) as easily as persuading a gaggle of girls and boys to do a dance in front of the school at Woodham Ferrers (*see page 70*).

In 1891, on 17 November, Fred formed another link in his close connection with Chelmsford. He stood at a by-election as a candidate for the Borough Council, and was elected, making him, at 33, the youngest member. The 'Essex County Chronicle' reported the occasion:

'Municipal Bye-Election at Chelmsford

On Tuesday an election took place at Chelmsford to fill the vacancy on the Town Council caused by the death of the late Mr. John Champ.

These 3 views illustrate Spalding's use of local people to fill dead ground in his photographs. Above is St. John's Green, Writtle, with the Cock & Bell in the foreground, the Star in the background, and the middle ground filled with one of his most elaborate pieces of 'business'. The co-operation of all these people suggests that even so close to the county town the taking of a photograph was still quite a novelty, but the scene is difficult to date – perhaps about 1890. The Cock & Bell still relies on a simple pictogram for its sign, said to derive from the small silver bells once presented as prizes at Shrove Tuesday cockfights.

St. Nicholas's church, Fyfield, in the early 1900s: this view was circulating as a postcard by 1905. Compare the children's games being played here with those at Woodham Ferrers school on page 70.

The Street at Little Waltham, looking east towards the Bell Inn, with Winckford Bridge just around the corner. The arrival of the telegraph in the late 1890s gives an approximate date to this view, issued as a postcard after 1903. To this side of Dennis Beer's saddlery-cum-Post Office is a late medieval Wealden house, its recessed central hall now divided into 2 floors. This type of building is quite rare in Essex, and perhaps indicates some fifteenth-century Kentish carpenter making his way northwards.

The candidates were – Mr. Fred Spalding, photographer, and Mr. Jacob Dalton, working engineer; the latter standing for the fifth time as a labour representative. The polling took place at the Vestry Hall. Alderman Dutton was returning officer. Messrs. A. J. Furbank and T. J. Smee were the presiding officers, and Messrs. H. M. Saltmarsh and H. G. Rogers the poll clerks. The returning officer liberally entertained the officials during the day. No great interest was manifested in the election, and the poll was light and uneventful. The agents and committee of each candidate worked hard for success. Mr. Spalding had several vehicles scouring the ward, but Mr. Dalton relied, as at former elections, on the support of the working people, 'who were not ashamed to walk'. Mr. J. Barker acted as honorary election agent for Mr. Spalding, and Mr. G. J. Hockley for Mr. Dalton. The counting took place at the Corn Exchange, and soon after nine o'clock Alderman Dutton announced from the balcony that the poll had resulted as follows:

Spalding	350
Dalton	262
Majority	88

He therefore declared Mr. Spalding elected. The announcement was received with cheers and hooting by a crowd assembled in the square. Councillor Spalding, in returning thanks for his election, said: 'Burgesses of the North ward, I sincerely thank you for sending me as one of your representatives on the Town Council. I especially thank the working men, for I know that it is to them in a great measure that I owe my position. (Cheers and cries of 'Shame'). During the last week I have met many unknown to me who promised to support me, and by the verdict of the poll I know they kept their word. (Cheers and hooting). I am not going to make you any rash and reckless promises, but I shall endeavour to do my duty independently of class, and for the benefit of the burgesses at large. (Cheers). My term of office is short – only a year – but I trust that at the end of that time I shall have gained many friends among those who have voted against me on this occasion.' (Cheers).' His expenses, published the following week, were eight pounds and nine pence!

So Fred continued on in business and in family life. His home life, according to his daughter Connie, was very happy and very hectic. He and his wife had 4 children: Kate Mary, popularly known as Gladys, born in March 1886; Constance Maude, known as Connie to all her friends, born in March 1889;

Frederick, born in October 1890; and Wilfred, born in January 1893.

One wonders if the children shown in his half-page advertisement in Daniels's guide to Chelmsford, published in 1908, were his own. A very modern-looking advertisement it was for those times, with lettering and photographs cut out and re-photographed on a neutral ground.

Improvements in the art of photography made Fred's life easier, or at least allowed him to cover more territory – as the advertisement shows. Dry gelatin plates could now be bought ready-prepared from commercial companies like Eastman and Kodak, and kept, after the photograph was taken, for development in a specially equipped dark room. The 'Essex Weekly News' from as early as 1908 was using portraits by Spalding's to add interest to articles on local personalities – all too often as obituaries!

Fred is remembered as starting the day at the shop, checking the smooth operation of the fancy goods repository and the productions of the dark room, dashing out in the horse and trap to fulfil commissions, popping across to the Corn Exchange to supervise arrangements for his latest promotion of a concert or similar entertainment, then checking his slides for his own presentation of Chelmsford's history to a local group. At the same time there was always some item of council business to be attended to. And whenever he had a moment free he would be seen in his workshop making the beautiful inlaid furniture and marquetry work of which only his family was aware.

There was a lighter side even to his work for the council. In 1908 the 'Essex Weekly News' reported on 6 March that 'the principal business at the meeting of the Chelmsford Ratepayers' Association was the further consideration of the most suitable site for the proposed public convenience'. 83 High Street had been suggested, but a petition had been got up favouring Tindal Square. 'Mr. John Bond (whose shop was nearer 83 than Tindal Square) said a convenience at the High Street site would be an insult to shop-keepers: and incidentally referring to the statue of Judge Tindal in Tindal Square, he described it as a hideous structure. If it was pulled down

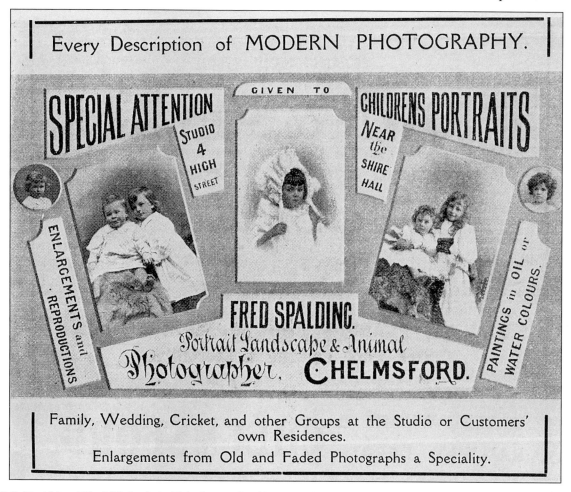

H. G. Daniels's guidebook 'Chelmsford with its Surroundings' in 1908 included this charming evidence of Spalding's talents in portrait photography.
Reproduced by courtesy of Chelmsford Library

and given to some farmer to put in his fields, no crow would come there. . . . Mr. W. Cowell . . . pointed out that Tindal Square was crowded with people on market days. What would happen if a pig or bullock found its way into the convenience?'

What of Councillor Spalding? Ever the peacemaker, the diplomat, he is quoted as saying that he would not oppose anything which was thought to be for the interests of the town. So the conveniences came to Tindal Square, with Judge Tindal turning his back to them!

In the same issue of the 'Weekly News', the anonymous writer under the name of 'The Deemster' asked why Chelmsford did not have a Photographic Society. Photography had passed out of the stage when it was mainly represented by misguided enthusiasts who spoilt good plates with grotesque caricatures of their friends and used bad language in the dark room. The possibilities of photography were 'widening every year, not only from the standpoint of art, but also commercially . . .'

So the Photographic Society was conceived, but Fred, as far as I can tell, would have none of it. His reputation, greatly enhanced by the commissions from the Prince of Wales, brought ever-increasing demand and I am sure his expertise

Every description of Modern Photography.

FRED SPALDING,

PORTRAIT, LANDSCAPE & ANIMAL PHOTOGRAPHER.

STUDIO :

4, High Street, Chelmsford.

Family, Wedding, Cricket and other Groups at the Studio or customers' Residences.

Enlargements from old & faded Photographs a Speciality

Spalding's advertisement in the second edition of Daniels's guidebook, 1909, moved from children to animals. This dramatic shot raises suspicions of photographic trickery, but the trick – if any – is not easy to detect.

had long since rendered 'dark room damnations' unnecessary. And his evenings were already taken up, in any case. In May 1908, when the Honourable Mrs. Greville got artistes together to present three plays at the Corn Exchange, to raise funds for the Danbury Church organ, we read, tucked away at the bottom of a glowing review, that 'the general arrangements were in the hands of Mr. Fred Spalding of Chelmsford'. And the photograph of Miss Phyllis Greville as a chamber maid, which headed the review, was taken by none other than Mr. Fred Spalding. It must have given Fred great satisfaction on opening his local paper that Friday morning to see his name shown twice, proving his expertise in two quite different fields of activity.

He was an all-round man, and by now a well known city father. He had continued as a councillor largely, I think, because he was assiduous in his attention to council business and popular with the electorate.

And he was a man of some presence, handsome and lean with clean features and naturally wavy hair. Now it was turning white it gave him added dignity, a dignity which was very appropriate for, at the meeting of 29 January 1913 Councillor Fred Spalding was, by 19 votes to 1, elected an alderman.

Then came the war and many changes, sacrifices, scarcities. Fred's sons went off to help their country. Fred, the elder, came back safely as a trained pilot and lieutenant in the R.A.F.. Wilfred was gassed on the Western Front and his injuries lasted the rest of his life, though he bravely took up a place in the business.

And what of the daily life of that now flourishing business? I was lucky enough to find, living in retirement in Chelmsford, a lady who had come up from the west country to work for Spalding's. She told me:

'I came to Chelmsford in November 1919. On arrival at Chelmsford station I was met by a porter with a hand barrow to carry my luggage and he took me straight to the High Street shop where I was interviewed by Mr. Spalding. I then went down Crane Court to Crane Court House which was where three or four of Spalding's employees lived in and Miss Spalding, sister of Frederick Spalding, ran the house for him and looked after the assistants, and we had a woman who used to come in and help her. In the evening the girls said 'Shall we go and look at the shops?' and we went up Moulsham Street and I was horrified to find there was only one street. I had come from Gloucester and when I asked where the rest of the shops were, they

14

said 'there aren't any more'. So I phoned my sister and said 'I don't think I shall be here longer than six months', but when I got into the shop and got working with the girls there I quite liked it.

'In the morning we used to get all the photographs that had been developed the day before in the dark room and they were all put out to dry and we had to dry these in the morning and straighten them and they all had to be backed with a tissue for dry mounting. That was one of my jobs – dry mounting and trimming and mounting actually on the mounts the photographs that were there, and of course there was always finishing to do, what was called spotting and retouching from negatives which we did daily because they all had to go along to the dark room to be printed.

'During the afternoon there were all sorts of things to do, mounting and sorting out the orders and getting them all in order. That was the daily routine, almost the same thing every day. But the thing is, it was not boring as you think it might be, because there were always so many different faces turning up – in the photographs, you see.'

People who had their photographs taken, she thought, were the better off, 'from Goldlay House and places like that. Of course photography was an expensive business, as it still is. We got a lot of people who wanted their children photographed before they grew up, and of course, outside photography which Mr. Spalding senior did. He was very good with horses. We did a lot for farmers, a lot of dairy work and farm work. There was nearly always something going on outside and Mr. Spalding senior was doing that, and Fred, when he came back from the R.A.F., took over the studio and carried on with that lot. Wilfred, of course, was the manager of the fancy goods and toy shop and although his health was not very grand, managed to carry on quite nicely. He was gassed in the War and he was very badly knocked about, and his face was badly damaged. He didn't have a lot of work to do but he had got a lot of staff to look after. And that was the general rule of the day. We used to work all day Saturday and leave at 6 o'clock, and we had Wednesday, I think, half day.'

Asked about the retouching that she spoke of, she said that it was done on the negative itself. 'A camera magnifies the defects and people don't want to look too old or too young, so you had to make sure you got the right touch for them according to their age, and on the negative, perhaps there were spots or eyebrows or things

that wanted tickling up a bit and that was what I did. When the proofs were sent out, some people were agreeably surprised.' This was skilled work: she said that she had been apprenticed for 3 years in Gloucester and after her apprenticeship was up she decided she wanted to go further afield. 'When my cousin knew I was coming to Chelmsford he told me not to go there as 'it's the last place they made and they've not finished it yet!' Funnily enough, he was stationed in Oaklands during the War and that was how he knew so much about it.'

'My job,' she said, 'was finishing and retouching, that was what we were classed as, finishers and retouchers. Fred Spalding added the birds and sometimes other items to the photographs. I well remember that Fred Spalding, the young one, used to do a lot of the Chelmsford Operatic when they first started, when Bellamy the chemist and all those were in it, and he did a picture of Peggy Green. She was supposed to be in one of these plays and she was flying through the air, but to get this, Fred lay her on a stool and took a photograph of her like that, and then turned the negative so she was flying through the air and of course she had never been there at all. He did a lot with the Operatic. Yearly to start with but twice yearly after that.'

I asked her, as she had had experience as an apprentice in Gloucester and was in a position to judge down the years, if she would say that Fred Spalding was a good photographer, and she replied that he was: 'he was very good with finishing and all that detail'. Mr. Spalding must have been satisfied with her work as she was there for 13 years and 9 months.

What was life like in those 13 years? Was Mr. Spalding a good employer? 'Yes, quite good but not very generous. In fact a friend of mine who had also worked in the shop . . . was talking about Spalding. I said 'I wonder what wage I got, I should think it was about £10 a month', so she said 'you were lucky. I got half a crown a week.' She was not really the buyer, but one of the head ones in the Stationery. She said that when she had been there a little while and asked for a rise, Mr. Wilfred Spalding said, 'Oh, you've spoilt it all. I was going to give it to you anyway'. Some of my money had to go towards my keep. I think £5 a month I gave to Miss Spalding to keep me and £5 a month I had to myself to spend as I liked. That was all I got.' However, the staff did 'get an occasional trip out. Mr. Spalding was very good. He invited us when he was made Freeman of the Borough and when he was Mayor the staff used to be invited.'

I asked if Mr. Spalding ever spoke to her

about his interest in local history. When he went out and brought some of these photographs back, she must have wondered where they were taken. 'Yes, well of course he had got all these things sort of tabulated and he would ask me, for example, to find him so and so of Moulsham Street, and you had to be fairly well up in it or you didn't know where to find the thing. He was very well up in old Chelmsford and what he didn't know about it wasn't really worth knowing. He had a very good filing system of all the local photographs and postcards. Funnily enough, they had a big Stationery Department and one of the buyers had stocked up with post-cards, there were boxes and boxes of them, and the staff used to buy these a bit cheaper. I still remember that I sent several to my friends and aunts and they said 'isn't there ever any daylight in Chelmsford?' It was always Chelmsford by moonlight!' She thought this was one of Mr. Spalding's tricks. He had reversed the negative, making it dark where it should be light, and drawn in a moon to achieve this novel effect.

Did she recall what it was like to have your photograph taken in Mr. Spalding's place in those days? She said that 'you had to be propped up and have your head just right and you had to have your shoulders right and every-thing had to be just so. To keep the people still at times you had to prop their heads up. Later on they got reflex cameras instead of the great big tripod thing that Mr. Spalding used to use. It was not a daylight studio. It was artificial light and for flashlight they used to have this great big thing that exploded.' As for making proofs of the photographs 'there was a place opposite the Saracen's Head which we used to call the Deck and all the frames were put out in there with proofs in and printed by daylight. You had to be careful to get them the right density and then they had to be packed up and sent to the customers, but of course, they had to be kept out of daylight then or they all faded again and you couldn't see them. The customers then had to choose the photographs they liked and bring back the proofs. You used to get quite good orders from them.

'Of course, Spalding's never made any money. Trade was always bad, or something, but still, they did quite well, I know. There were one or two other photographers in the town, but I think that at that time Mr. Spalding was classed as the leading one. There were others that followed on afterwards, several of which I know of, but I think he was the one, he had got it all at his fin-gertips. When Wilfred took on the studio, that was wonderful and he really was very clever

with that.

'The shop generally, selling all those gifts, did better business than the photography side because it went into gramophone records. They had what they called a gramophone room and they went into all sorts of fancy goods and an

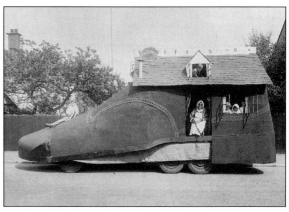

Mother Hubbard makes her appearance on a Spalding float at one of Chelmsford's carnivals, urging onlookers 'to help your hospital shoe the debt away'.

enormous range of toys. In fact, they used to enter the carnivals.'

Her memories of the carnival season included – apparently – two of Spalding's own floats. 'One year they had a float representing Old Mother Hubbard and I went on it. They wanted a slogan to go on top of the ark and I said, 'Ark, the animals all sing the praises of Spalding the toy shop king'. That was put over the top of the ark and inside I was Old Mother Hubbard. Spalding spent a lot of time with that. Much more than he should have done, I think. That was probably because of his connections with the town, as a councillor, that he felt he must support them. Wilfred did most of that. They used to have photographs taken of it and they were all displayed round about.'

Fred jogged on in business and in leisure, occupying his time fully and profitably. He was very interested in cricket – particularly in trying to establish a county ground in Chelmsford – and he continually worked to raise funds for the hospital, acting for several years as chairman of the Hospital Carnival Committee. Other little thoughtfulnesses come to light. A minute of the Training of Disabled Ex-Servicemen Sub-Committee for 2 September 1921 reveals that 'recreation equipment', cricket stumps and accoutrements, were all donated by 'Spalding'.

From amongst his fellow aldermen Fred was elected mayor for the three years from 1922 to 1924. What a busy life for a 64-year old! His life-long attachment to the parish church – now the cathedral – was celebrated then with a brass alms dish which he gave, simply engraved 'Cathedral Church of St. Mary. Frederick Spalding. Mayor 1922/23/24.' It marked his happiness in serving God and his fellow men.

The years passed. Fred continued, seemingly indestructible. In 1926, on 25 October, when he was 67, he sat on the Bench as a Justice of the Peace. He was also a governor of the Grammar School, and a director of three building and assurance societies. Yet he also found time to act as master of the Masonic Lodge of Good Fellowship, and was giving up evenings to provide lantern lectures on the town he loved so much.

1927 was a sad year. He was approaching 70, but his son Frederick was carried off by illness aged only 36. Wilfred bravely stepped into the photographic side of the business and managed very well despite his own war wounds.

In 1929, the County Library – then but three years old – became for several years one of Fred's tenants, using rooms he owned down Crane Court.

Proof of Fred's endless interest in the town and its institutions is that little book I have mentioned – the record of his talk at the Y.M.C.A. in 1930 when he was 71. How many of us would like to manage a projector and slides and talk at the same time at that age? But as far as business went, Fred was passing into retirement and Wilfred had the staff to cope with both sides of the business.

On 18 December 1933, and in his 76th year, Alderman Spalding was made an Honorary Freeman of the Borough – a public appreciation of his service to the town stretching over 42 years. The local paper says it all:

'On Monday a special meeting of the Chelmsford Town Council presented the Honorary Freedom of the Borough to Alderman Frederick Spalding, J.P., 'in recognition of his long, faithful, and devoted services as a Councillor and Alderman since 17th November, 1891'. This was the fourth name added to the roll of Freemen.

'The presentation took place in the County Room of the Shire Hall, which the Corporation, robed, entered in procession, and where the Mayor (Councillor S. C. Taylor) took the chair, with Alderman Spalding at his right side. There was a large attendance of friends and well-wishers, including the only other surviving Freeman, Mr. Walter Cowell.

'The proceedings opened with prayer by the Mayor's Chaplain. The Mayor then recited the works of Alderman Spalding, who had been a Councillor from 1891 to 1913, and an Alderman from 1913 to date, and is still serving. They hoped indeed to have the benefit of their

friend's good counsel and co-operation for many more years to come on behalf of the general well-being of their town. Alderman Spalding's name would stand out as one of the best servants the Borough of Chelmsford ever had. During his years of Mayoralty, 1922–1924, he was a great worker for all that tended to the betterment of the burgesses, while his kind heart had done good that was known only to a few. In honouring Alderman Spalding they were honouring themselves, and they wished him many happy years in which to enjoy his well-earned distinction. (Applause). They had not given away the freedom of the Borough wholesale in Chelmsford – it had been looked upon as an almost sacred thing. The Borough was incorporated in 1888, but until last year only two men had been granted the freedom of the Borough. 'When Alderman Spalding first took his seat on the Chelmsford Town Council on November 17th, 1891,' added the Mayor, 'it was my father as Mayor who greeted him. When he took his seat as an Alderman in 1913 he was greeted by my brother, the late Alderman George Taylor. To-night the privilege falls to me of handing him the freedom of this borough.'

'The Mayor then asked the Town Clerk (Mr. G. E. Barford) to read the resolution of the Council of October 25th last, agreeing to admit the Alderman to the Freedom. This done, the Mayor called upon Alderman J. O. Thompson, O.B.E., J.P., the senior Alderman, to move a resolution.

'Alderman Thompson said it sounded a serious thing to be styled the senior Alderman, but the position gave him the privilege, which he highly prized, of saying a few words on a memorable occasion and of moving:

That the Honorary Freedom of the Borough be now presented to Alderman Frederick Spalding, J.P., in accordance with the resolution of the Council of this Borough.

Their motto that day was not 'Many minds, one heart', but 'One mind, one heart', for that rare ceremony was devised in true friendship to honour another distinguished servant of the place. By an ambition rightly directed, Alderman Spalding had for over 42 years contributed to the advantage and happiness of the people of Chelmsford, upon that Council and in various other ways, some of them mentioned by the Mayor. To paraphrase some well-known words:

Fred Spalding is a citizen
Of credit and renown,

A noted servant eke is he
Of famous Chelmsford town.

He was a man of great good feeling, sincere, sensitive, warm-hearted. He had bravely achieved this honour by his own merit and steadfastness. He had fought hard in many good causes; worked hard for many good things. In particular of late he had striven for 'more light', and to preserve such ancient monuments as they had left to them. The old Conduit was one of the last remaining, and, having been a noted cyclist and now a good, upright pedestrian, he wanted the Conduit to remain, for he found that the driving of motor cars generally, with all respect to Councillor Bellamy, was like the driving of Jehu, the son of Himshi – 'for he driveth furiously'. (Laughter). He (Alderman Thompson) had spoken of ambition rightly directed. What was ambition?

'True ambition there alone resides
Where justice vindicates and wisdom guides.'

And who were the real Free Men? Those who were

'True to the law of right, as warmly prone
To grant another's as maintain their own.'

Frederick Spalding answered that description and his would be a worthy name upon their scroll of fame. (Applause).

'The motion having been unanimously carried, the Oath was administered, whereby the new Freeman swore that he would well and truly serve our Sovereign Lord the King, and as a free and franchised man of the Borough, 'preserve the common peace and tranquillity of the said Borough so far as in me lieth, and if I know of any unlawful assemblies against the State thereof I will forthwith disclose the same to the Mayor for the time being, whom I will aid by my best counsel and advice, and I will defend the customs and privileges of this Borough in every just and lawful cause.'

'Alderman Spalding having signed the Freeman's Roll, the Mayor presented the certificate of Freedom (together with a casket prepared for its reception by order of the Corporation), and tendered Alderman Spalding the right hand of fellowship as a Freeman. His Worship, on behalf of Freeman Cowell, also handed a bouquet to Alderman Spalding's daughter, Miss Constance Spalding.

'Alderman Spalding, in reply, said he felt deeply moved by the kind references which had been made to his service on the Council. That it was one of the proudest moments of his life – to have added his name to the roll of Honorary

Freemen was the greatest honour his native place could give him. He treasured not only the distinction conferred upon him by his fellow members of the Council but also the good wishes which so many of the townspeople had expressed to him since the proposal for that evening's ceremony was made. He knew that honour came from the whole of the town. (Applause). Continuing, the Alderman said he had given the borough the best service he had been capable of during the last 42 years; it was a big part of anybody's life, and now it was a pleasant reflection to know that what he had been able to do was appreciated. His biggest regret was that his wife, to whom he owed whatever success he had achieved, was unable to be present, but he rejoiced to see his children and grandchildren present. Chelmsford was a town growing in importance every year as a shopping centre, an industrial centre, and a residential centre. He was proud to be an old Chelmsfordian. Every year of his work on the Council had its pleasant memories besides its hard work. Apart from its modern aspect, Chelmsford had a store of historic places which it was their duty carefully to preserve in order that future generations might find therein links with the past which would tell them something of the town's earlier days. 'I shall continue to serve my native borough as long as I have the power in me,' added the Alderman, amid applause. 'Our borough has a wonderful reputation, and I am certain it will continue to prosper.'

'The proceedings concluded with the singing of the National Anthem. At the invitation of Freeman Spalding the company afterwards partook of refreshments in the Grand Jury Room.'

So Fred headed into retirement, though he continued performing his duties as an Alderman. We can find a neat summary of his life down to 1935 in a 'Who's Who in Essex', published in that year:

'SPALDING, Frederick (Alderman), J.P. Retired. 'Wimborne', Chelmsford.

Born 1858 at Chelmsford. Son of late Frederick Spalding.

Educated privately.

Married 1885, Emma A., daughter of the late C. D. Darby.

Elected member of Chelmsford Town Council, 1891, forty-three years continual service, again elected, 1934, for six years; Alderman of the Borough (Father of the Council); Justice of the Peace for Essex, 1926; Mayor of the Borough, 1922–23 and 24 (three years); Hon. Freeman of the Borough, 1933; elected representative of the Chelmsford Bench of Magistrates at the Guild Hall, London; Commissioner of Taxes and a Commissioner of Appeal; Chairman of Chelmsford & Essex Hospital Carnival, raising £7,300 to New Building Fund; introduced County Cricket at Chelmsford in 1925; first President, and Chairman of Executive Committee since 1925; started St. John Ambulance in Chelmsford; Hon. Treasurer for Chelmsford Division (District 10), 1926–31; Governor, King Edward VI Grammar School; Ann Johnson's Bounty; Elementary Schools; and Governor of Guy's Charity for the Borough; in early days won many cycling prizes.'

Note that the extract quoted was from a 'Who is Who' of 1935. Fred was still an 'Is-going' and not a 'Has-been', but he was being slowed up by advancing years. The death of his wife was a great blow to him. The 'Essex Chronicle' carries the sad note: 'SPALDING – On January 14th, 1941, Emma Agnes, the loved wife of Frederick Spalding, Wimborne, London Road, passed peacefully to her rest.' He was further saddened by the death of his brother Herbert less than a fortnight later.

Fred himself lived on in grand and honourable old age down to 1947, but falling ill in the winter he died on Sunday, 2 February, at his home in London Road. The obituaries in the local newspapers were long and appreciative:

'Mr. Frederick Spalding, three times Mayor of Chelmsford, a Freeman of the borough, and a member of the Town Council for the record period of 54 years, died on Sunday at his residence, Wimborne, London Road. He was 88.

'From the time he was a young man until recent years, Mr. Spalding rendered conspicuous and devoted service to his native town. Even in his later years he was remarkably active in mind and body, and he possessed a charming personality. Of him it may truly be said that he grew old gracefully.

'Mr. Spalding was the son of the late Mr. Frederick Spalding, who established the business of photographer in Tindal Square and he was born in Duke Street. His long and unbroken service on the Town Council first as the youngest member and later as its 'father' was regarded as a record in Essex municipal history; it began at a by-election on November 17 1891, only three years after the incorporation of the borough. In those days elections were marked by considerable strife and intense rivalry, but Mr. Spalding headed the poll against opposition which declared he 'hadn't an earthly' and he was subsequently continuously returned by the burgesses, serving as a councillor until 1913.

'Chelmsford, its history, associations, features and traditions, were as dear almost as life itself to Mr. Spalding, who strove by every means in his power to see that Chelmsford occupied its rightful place as the County Town of Essex. He was the recognised authority on old Chelmsford, collecting a wealth of information on its industry, and he was always deeply grieved when century old landmarks disappeared. He fought a long battle to save the demolition of the conduit which formerly stood at Springfield Road corner, but it was eventually moved to Tower Gardens (*see page 27*). Mr. Spalding also opposed the removal of the old Russian gun which, after standing outside the Shire Hall since 1858, found a new home in Oaklands Park (*see page 26*).

'Mr. Spalding was a lifelong friend of the Cathedral. Born under its shadows, christened and confirmed within its walls, he served for many years as a sidesman. In 1924, during his Mayoralty, he presented to the Cathedral an inscribed brass alms dish which is still in use.

'His charitable interests included: Chelmsford Hospital, the Treloar Home for Crippled Children, and the former Chelmsford Christmas Cheer Fund, by which those who had fallen on bad times were assured of a good Christmas dinner. He was Chairman of Chelmsford Carnival for several years.

'Cricket was one of Mr. Spalding's lifelong interests, and he was always to be seen, until his health prevented it, at the Chelmsford festival which he had himself done much to bring about. He had been chairman of the festival committee; in fact he held the office for the festival last year, the first after the war and it was a deep disappointment to Mr. Spalding that his health would not allow him to attend. Athletics had also been one of his great interests and in his younger days he was reputed to be one of the fastest riders in Essex on the old 'ordinary' high bicycle (*see page 6*).

'Mr. Spalding had been a Justice of the Peace since 1926 and until increasing age made it difficult to attend regularly sat on the Chelmsford Bench. In Freemasonry he was the oldest member of the Lodge of Good Fellowship, No. 276, being a Past Master; for some years he was a governor of King Edward the Sixth School, Chelmsford . . . .

'In later years, Mr. Spalding's birthday was the occasion for many of his friends and associates to visit his home in London Road to toast the health of one of the town's grandest Old Chelmsfordians.'

By May 1947 Fred's will had been published.

He left to his grandsons, Martyn and Antony Spalding, his collection of photographs of old and modern Chelmsford, asking that they should be exhibited to the public from time to time, 'so that future generations may see a pictorial record of the great changes which have come about in the borough'.

His wish, at least in part, is fulfilled, even though much of the Spaldings' work – their portraits in particular – survives now only in the private hands for whom it was produced. New examples continue to turn up, and while the collecting goes on, there cannot be an exhaustive guide to the world of the Spaldings. But even this small selection, we hope, gives something of its flavour, and offers us all a glimpse into an era that has quite vanished, except for some dark specks of silver on some small panes of glass.

Stan Jarvis

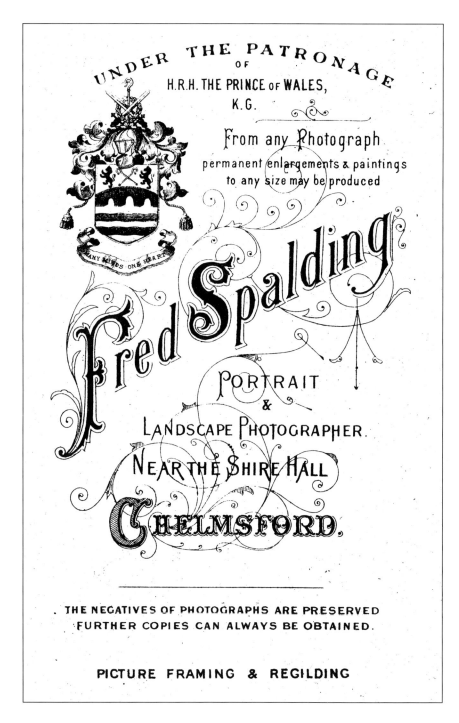

The mounts used by Victorian photographers are often highly decorative, and sometimes slightly misleading. This example from the Spalding archive, incorporating the borough arms of 1889, and celebrating Spalding's royal connection, supports a print of an event in 1903 – two years after the Prince of Wales had ascended the throne as Edward VII.

The Changing Face of Chelmsford

An aerial view of central Chelmsford, taken just before the Second World War. The new block of County Hall rises palely over what was still a townscape of the nineteenth and earlier centuries. Today, almost all the buildings on the left hand side of the photograph, and many on the right, have disappeared. Even in 1907, the 'County Standard' – a Colchester paper – had noted acidly that 'Chelmsford may be old, but the visitor *who tries to discover traces of its past glories has a disappointing time', and the process of destruction continued through and beyond Fred Spalding's lifetime. His regret was expressed in a sequence of photographs, deliberately pointing up the changes in the face of the town.*

An early view of the north side of Tindal Square, Chelmsford, taken in the late 1860s. In the centre is the Spalding shop, and on its roof the glass studio – a necessity for photographers before the days of effective artificial lighting. In his old age, Fred remembered standing up there as a boy, watching the fire that destroyed Ridley's corn mill in 1869. At this time, Tindal Square was still a market-place: the posts were not to stop carts parking on the pavements, but to allow ropes to be strung between them on market days to create stalls for horses.

Almost the same view, but taken in the late 1920s. The Spaldings have moved on, and their studio looks rather dilapidated, but the chemist next door is advertising 'films developed & printed': the age of amateur photography has truly arrived. There are marked contrasts between the restrained shop fronts of the 1860s and the blaring advertisements of this scene, and between the quiet cobbled square and this space laid out for the convenience of motor vehicles. The square's modern appearance only remains to be completed by a vast increase in traffic, and by the replacement of the retail traders by financial services.

Tindal Square in about 1906, showing on the extreme left the original Spalding shop and studio – now Godfrey's, rope and tent makers – and on the extreme right the windows of its replacement. Admiring these was not always a safe occupation: in 1914, a runaway horse plunged through the furthest window, and a bystander – a watchman from the Marconi works – was fatally injured against the iron railings. The Shire Hall of 1792, bracketed by the 2 phases of Spalding's professional life, was especially dear to him. When the interior was drastically altered in 1936 he protested that the vestibule was left looking 'like the entrance of a modern cinema'.

Edward VII is proclaimed King from the steps of the Shire Hall on 25 January 1901, to a representative gathering of Chelmsfordians. The little straw hats seen on many ladies' heads were a feature of turn-of-the-century fashion. Just visible in the doorway are the plumes of the High Sheriff of Essex, Henry Collings Wells. A thorough-going Chelmsford man, from the Wells & Perry brewing firm, he sparked an inter-urban incident by declining to send a copy of the proclamation to Colchester Corporation so that they could proclaim the new King too. The resulting acrid correspondence reached even the columns of 'The Times'.

One of Chelmsford Corporation's constant concerns was the widening of the town's roads, to cope with ever-growing volumes of traffic. Here, improvement comes to Duke Street in the 1930s. With the removal of part of Webber's jeweller's shop – the site of a smithy in Spalding's youth – a breach was made through to the cathedral church of St. Mary, where he and his children were christened, and where he served as a sidesman for many years. Except for an influx of building societies, the street scene thus created survives largely intact. Notice the milk cart in the extreme right of the earlier photograph: Spalding seldom focussed directly on the ordinary life of the street, but sometimes it does gleam through.

On 4 July 1903, Chelmsford took on an unusually military air for the visit of 2 Field Marshals: Earl Roberts, victor over the Boers, to open the new Volunteers' Drill Hall, and Sir Evelyn Wood – son of a vicar of Cressing – to become the borough's first honorary freeman. Spalding's photographs show the expectant crowds in Tindal Square, and the official party at the Drill Hall. Roberts is in the centre with the Mayor, George Taylor; the plumed figure to the left is the Earl of Warwick, Lord Lieutenant of Essex; and to the right, beside the mace, is Captain Showers, the Chief Constable, making a rare appearance in official dress. The small boys are from the Felsted School Cadet Corps.

HOUNDS AT CHELMSFORD.

A meet of foxhounds at Chelmsford is an event which one never sees nowadays, and was a very rare occurrence years ago when the County Town was more the centre of country life than it is to-day. I notice that the Essex Union pack selected the High-st. as the rendezvous on the last Saturday of January, 1911, following the annual ball which was held at the Shire Hall the previous night. The morning was gloriously fine and sunny, and the scene was picturesque, with plenty of life and colour. According to the account of the meet published in the "Essex Weekly News" at the time, it was over a quarter of a century since the Essex Union last met opposite the Saracen's Head. I think I am correct in stating that they have not done so since. At any rate, I cannot recall an occasion. Chelmsford, it seems, is a kind of a "buffer kingdom" for hunting people—or, at any rate, it was in those days. According to the arrangements then existing, the boundaries of the Essex, the East Essex, and the Essex Union countries joined in the County Town. Formerly Moulsham Thrift Wood, near Galleywood—which was drawn on the occasion of the meet in 1911—was regarded as a neutral covert every other month by the Essex Union and the Essex, but it has not been visited for many years by the latter pack. It lies, of course, in the Essex Union country, which is bounded by the Navigation and the old London-Colchester road.

In 1911 Tindal Square saw the first meeting of the Essex Union Hunt in Chelmsford in nearly 30 years (and, thought Fred in old age, the last). The territory of the Essex Union extended south-eastwards from the town, and was to suffer sadly from urban sprawl. This is also one of the first photographs to show fully the cluster of official buildings which had edged private residents from this side of the square: Barclays Bank (1905), the Post Office (1908), and the turreted police station (1906).

The coronation of George V in June 1911 called for further celebrations. The Deputy Mayor (the Mayor was in Westminster Abbey) led a carriage procession to the recreation ground where, at the exact moment of crowning, the miracle of wireless allowed him to send a signal to Marconi's 230-foot mast in Hall Street, on which the Union Jack was then raised. A further sign of progress is the arc lamp seen here on the traffic island in Tindal Square: in 1890, thanks to the presence of Crompton's Arc Works, Chelmsford became a pioneer in the use of electricity for street lighting. Less commonly recorded is the fact that for some years after 1920 the town reverted to gas lamps, in an attempt to save money.

The earliest surviving view down Chelmsford High Street, probably taken in the 1870s. Fred himself, in his later lecturing days, used this picture to jog his memories – for instance about Medlicott the tallow-chandler's, down on the left, with its smell of hot fat and 'candles of all sizes hanging from the ceiling. You had to take care to dodge the rows, unless you wanted your hat knocked off or your hair well greased.' Most striking now are the emptiness of the roads (made up with a loose mixture of stones and gravel) and sobriety of the facades. The High Street was still home to some of the town's professional classes: next to the Saracen's Head stood the premises of John Champ, the teetotal wine merchant whose shop – and seat on the Borough Council – were later taken over by Fred Spalding.

A later view down the High Street, with Spalding's shop now in place at numbers 4 & 5. Post-dating his move from Tindal Square in the early 1890s, it must have been taken before 1907. On a foggy February night in that year, practical jokers fired a blank charge from the 36-pounder Russian cannon which since 1858 had stood before the Shire Hall, breaking 5 panes of glass and a street lamp. The next meeting of the Borough Council carried Spalding's motion asking for the cannon to be stopped up. Until its removal to Oaklands Park in 1937, it was a focal point in the town, and 'speaking from the Gun' was a common position for local orators.

The Spaldings' earliest surviving view of the lower end of Chelmsford High Street, probably taken in about 1865. On the Springfield Road corner, beside Madock's broom and brush makers (estab. 1860), is the vacant lot occupied until 1857 by the Black Boy Inn, a famous posting house. In front of it stands the conduit, first erected in Tindal Square in 1814, but moved to this site in 1851–2 in order to make way for the statue of Judge Tindal. An interesting feature of this plate is the ghostly shapes left on the slow wet collodion negative by pedestrians in motion.

The Saracen's Head Hotel, recorded under that name from 1539, was once one of Chelmsford's leading coaching inns. The hotel also has literary associations, for Anthony Trollope wrote in its smoking room, and lodged there when hunting with the Essex packs ('Essex was the chief scene of my sport . . . Few have investigated more closely than I have done the depth, and breadth, and water-holding capacities of an Essex ditch'). During the Second World War, as this photograph shows, the hotel was occupied by the American Red Cross. Spalding has even taken care to include a jeep for the full transatlantic effect.

King George V in Chelmsford High Street during the First World War, photographed from the window of Spalding's shop. The firms on the other side – Joseph Smith & Sons the drapers, Tindall & Jarrold the stationers, the Domestic Bazaar Company ('The Finest Selection In The World At One Price 6$\frac{1}{2}$d.'), and the saddlers Fitch & Son – fix the period close to the King's visit of October 1914, to inspect 15,000 men in training at Hylands Park. However, the 'Essex Weekly News' reported that afterwards His Majesty did not continue as planned to the town, but motored straight back to London. Could a newspaper be wrong?

Even when the conduit was moved in 1851, the Board of Health wondered whether the High Street was wide enough to accommodate it. The years, and the growth in traffic, justified their fears. Councillor F. G. Smith, in 1925, expressed the view of the 'antis': 'it was a nuisance where it was. It was dirty, occupying too much room, should be a fountain, but was now nothing but an eyesore and a danger to traffic, used as a sort of advertising hoarding.' Alderman Spalding consistently spoke up for the conduit as 'part and parcel of Chelmsford', but in 1940 resistance crumbled and the conduit was taken down and removed to Tower Gardens.

The Half Moon Inn, at the junction of Chelmsford High Street and the New London Road, near the end of its long existence in the 1930s. Even in 1900, when the Half Moon still hung from the building, a local antiquary pointed it out sadly as a 'house about to be pulled down', but it sheltered for another generation behind a new shop front.

Chelmsford High Street in about 1908, its busy commercial life caught sharply by a dry plate: even the waggon advancing towards us can be identified as belonging to the Chelmsford Co-operative Industrial Society. On the right, Madock's continue to sell their brushes, but the Black Boy site has been filled by Barnard's Temperance Hotel of 1868. On the left, beyond the Baddow Brewery's Queen's Head, can just be seen the Rayleigh Arms, where until recently Fred Spalding's younger brother Arthur had been licensee. This bustling scene awaits only the arrival in force of motor vehicles to justify the anonymous judgement of 1918: 'the High Street of Chelmsford is rapidly becoming as risky to pedestrians as a crossing in Piccadilly or the Strand'.

One of the latest photographs in the collection is this view of the High Street just after the Second World War. The white bulk of Marks & Spencer's 'bazaar' of about 1930, and the arrival of Boots the Chemists on the Springfield Road corner, mark the advance of the multiple store. Many other shop fronts have been modernized, but the upper storeys remain relatively unaltered. The removal of the conduit, however, has hardly eased the traffic problem. The stage is set for the final solution of July 1992: complete pedestrianization.

High Street, Springfield Corner, 1930.

The transformation of the opposite corner of the Springfield Road between 1930 and 1932 demonstrated not only the pace of commercial development, but also the importance of price in making a sale during the Depression. The Fifty Shilling Tailors placed some particularly strident advertisements, for example this from March 1932: 'Amazing Scenes at Chelmsford. All British Tailoring Depot Crowded Out. Special Request from the Directors owing to the extraordinary crowds at the weekend . . .' for all who could to **avoid** shopping there on Fridays and Saturdays.

High Street, Springfield Corner, 1932.

28

The change illustrated by this pair of pictures occurred at the western end of Duke Street. These ramshackle shops, opposite the war memorial of 1923, were demolished in November 1933, one month after the foundation stone had been laid for the new library and civic offices beside it. They were replaced by the flat, patterned brickwork on the left of the second photograph. The tiny greengrocer's became a ladies hairdresser's; Pannell the fishmonger's gave way to a ladies outfitter's; and a grocer's shop replaced Jane Turner's 'fancy repository'.

Moulsham Street, Chelmsford, just before the First World War, showing J. G. Bond's furniture store at the old militia armoury; the Chelmsford Star Co-operative building of 1880; the high Wesleyan Methodist Church, 'in the Perpendicular style of Gothic, with several late Decorated features', *which in 1898 replaced the Cock Inn at the northern end of the stone bridge; and on the right the pitched roofs of the Cross Keys Inn, unoccupied for several years before in 1914 it was acquired by a cinema company, and shortly afterwards replaced by the Regent Theatre.*

Moulsham Street – with the Wesleyan Methodist Church just visible in the background – in about 1910. The forest of telephone wires and the electric arc lamps testify already to the advances of technology, and it would not be long before motor traffic chased these children off the main *roads. They may well have been pupils at St. John's Church School (out of shot behind the camera), to whom the Moulsham Street pump must have offered considerable temptations. Its main use, however, was in watering the dusty summer streets.*

The Friary in Moulsham Street, dating from about 1320, derived its name from the Dominican Priory which once stood on the site. Even when first photographed by Spalding in 1882, it carried the scars of an earlier round of demolition in about 1858, when Friars Gateway was removed and Friars Place driven through to the left.

This skeletal photograph of about 1931 is apparently all that remains of an early, radical and unsuccessful conservation project, in which Spalding took a hand, either to re-assemble the building in its entirety elsewhere, or to incorporate 'the more choice parts . . . in a Mayor's parlour in the projected new municipal buildings' (erected in 1933–4).

Neither plan found favour, and the Friary was reincarnated simply as a block of shops, set back to allow for road-widening. These in their turn have now given way to a later and larger road.

31

The Spotted Dog public house at 24 Tindal Street, Chelmsford, at about the time of the First World War. The town's commercial importance brought it a wealth of pubs, of which the greatest concentration lay here, on the site of the market founded in 1199. At this date the street still contained – besides the Spotted Dog – the Dolphin, the White Hart (just visible here to the right), the Bell and the Market House Inn. All but the last were pulled down in 1969–71, to make way for the High Chelmer Shopping Centre.

The New London Road, Chelmsford, in a view of the early 1900s measured up for use as a postcard. In the distance, beside the iron bridge over the Can, is the Congregational Chapel, opened in 1840; on the right, with the sharply angled roof (and with an interested policeman outside) is the Sunday School, built in 1867 to provide an alternative to meetings in the chapel's basement; and to this side is the yard of J. B. Slythe, monumental masons (estab. 1851). Nearly all the constituents of this view – trees and all – have gone. The chapel was demolished in 1969–70, when its members merged into the new Christ Church, and Parkway now runs across the centre of the picture. On its northern side, only a fragment of terrace with a balustrade now remains.

The lower-lying parts of Chelmsford were always poorly drained, but the events of August 1888 became notorious as the Great Flood. Spalding took a series of photographs of the main streets, ankle-deep in water, and also of this hole where the iron bridge had carried the New London Road across the River Can. The now somewhat superfluous notice on the right hand pier, warning traction engines against using the bridge, resulted from an incident 4 years before, when 2 engines belonging to Binney's of Ilford had shaken off a 3-foot section of girder. This more serious damage took longer to repair, the new bridge being opened only in November 1890.

A group portrait of the marshals who on 19 September 1888 shepherded through Chelmsford's streets a huge procession of 'men on horseback, men on foot, lucky ones in carriages, school children tired and restless, Volunteers anxious to 'step-out', Fire Brigades, mounted police, Hussars, Mayors and Aldermen' – all celebrating the grant of the borough charter. Fred Spalding's decorations were reported as 'making by far the most attractive show in [Tindal] Square', and he was among the 500 guests at a grand dinner in the Corn Exchange. He also took 14 photographs of the procession – none of which he seems to have kept.

The modern prison system was a nineteenth-century invention. A new 'convict gaol' at Springfield, replacing the old building beside Moulsham Bridge, opened in 1828. Successively enlarged, by 1899 – when the staff posed for this portrait – it had 361 cells, but later was to meet with such a shortage of convicts that it was mothballed from 1919 to 1930.

In the late nineteenth century, Chelmsford's population was growing at an average of 10% every decade. The question naturally arose of how to gather the new suburbs for Christ, and one answer was the mission room. This Edwardian congregation is grouped outside All Saints Mission, an iron church built in 1905 in the Broomfield Road, near Christy's engineering works, and served from St. Mary's parish church in the town centre.

In May 1899, Chelmsford Borough Fire Brigade proudly demonstrated its new fire escape, tall enough, it was said, to reach the borough's highest building. Propping the ladder against the side of the Corn Exchange, 8 fully-equipped firemen tested its strength by standing on it, and they then took it in turns to wheel it to and from the fire station in Market Road, rounding off the entertainment with one fireman carrying another from the roof, greatly to the delight of the crowd'. At this date the steam fire engine itself was still hauled by horse-power: a second engine was acquired in 1904, but only in 1918 did the council authorize trials with a Panhard motor to draw it along.

The Borough Fire Brigade seems to have held a special interest for Fred Spalding. In 1907, after Superintendent Farrow and his men had complained rather too vigorously of being 'interfered with' by their chief officer in tackling a fire at Messrs. Godfrey in Moulsham, a reorganization was proposed which in effect meant Farrow's dismissal. Councillor Spalding opposed the motion, drawing an allegation that some members 'were there for personal ends, or for personal friends'. 'Rot!' was his reply, but his opposition failed, and the whole brigade resigned in protest. Farrow, however, had the last laugh, being elected a borough councillor a few months later, and subsequently serving as chairman of the Fire Brigade Committee.

The shock of the Crimean War in the 1850s helped to spur the revival of the militia, the ancient – and in theory obligatory – citizen's army. The West Essex Militia, re-embodied in 1854 under Colonel Samuel Ruggles-Brise, was stationed at Chelmsford until 1879, when it moved to Warley Barracks. Here is the militia band in about 1860, drawn up beside their headquarters in Barrack Square. In the background, beyond the River Can, are the terraces of the New London Road. The militia was a very local force: this unit's surgeon, Dr. Gilson, was Spalding's predecessor at 5 High Street, and the bandmaster, Charles Byford, later sat with him on the Borough Council.

The laying of foundation stones has always attracted photographers, and Spalding was no exception. Here John Burrows, chairman of Essex County Council, lays the first stone of the new County Hall in Duke Street, Chelmsford, in 1933. The plans for County Hall had been completed 2 decades earlier, but constantly shelved for financial reasons. One of the buildings now demolished was the former George Inn, whose tenant Arthur Spalding (Fred's brother?) had received £350 from the council in 1913, for loss of fixtures and fittings on termination of his tenancy. By 1914, the inn's back parlour and back kitchen held the drawing staff of the County Architect. The new building of 1933, costing £22,000, had room for 290 staff, but further extensions were already contemplated.

Chelmsford's leading position in the new world of electrical engineering received military recognition during the Boer War. In early 1900, Major R. E. Crompton – of Crompton's Arc Works – was put in command of the Electrical Engineers Volunteer Corps. Some 50 strong, their role was to operate searchlights for night fighting, while half the men, it was reported, 'will be provided with bicycles, on which are fitted drums containing fine telegraph or telephone wire, and by this system it is hoped that over any rideable ground three cyclists can lay a mile of field telegraph in fifteen minutes'. At a grand farewell dinner in the Shire Hall, Spalding provided a show of lantern slides of the British commanders, culminating in a portrait of Queen Victoria. 'The company cheered themselves hoarse at sight of the venerable, kindly face . . .'

Out and About in Essex

County Alderman William Glenny (1839–1923), for 20 years chairman of the Romford Board of Guardians, puts his trowel to their new infirmary at Romford workhouse – later Oldchurch Hospital – in 1891.

Rochford in the early 1900s, looking along West Street towards Market Square, with the Marlborough Head Inn on our right. The saddler's shop on the opposite side of the road passed from Thomas to Edward McBryer just before the First World War.

Chipping Ongar High Street between about 1902 and 1909, looking south over the wide space which until recently had accommodated the town's ancient market and fair. The fair, and probably the market too, was suppressed in 1892, and in 1896–7 the old town hall, where they had lately been held, was demolished. The space where it stood lies in the centre of the photograph, to this side of the row of shops. In the last winter of the First World War, with increasingly scarce foodstuffs now rationed, the local branch of the Farmers' Union tried to revive the market, in order to make sure that local meat supplies went to local people, but the authorities apparently vetoed the scheme.

Ongar

Another postcard view of the early 1900s, taken in The Borough, Chipping Ongar's tiny industrial area below Ongar Bridge. Just out of shot to the right is the brickworks (closed in 1917), while over the cottages to the left rise the works of the Ongar Gas Company (closed in 1934). At this time,

the company – which itself disappeared by amalgamation in 1910 – lit Ongar's public lamps, like the one in the foreground, between 1 September and 30 April, at a cost in gas of £2 2s. per lamp, plus £3 7s. 6d. for cleaning and painting.

The nonconformist minister's house at Great Leighs, placed provokingly at the gates of the rectory. The parish was the scene of a polite contest between the rector and the Tritton family, the major landowners, one of whose members in 1854 built a non-sectarian chapel on the road between the rectory and the church. Which minister this is remains unclear, but the photograph's mount carries Spalding's Tindal Square address, suggesting a date no later than the early 1890s, just when the young lady's boater was coming into fashion. It is easy to see in the 2 central figures here William Howieson, the Scots Congregationalist, and his wife Ellen from Newcastle-upon-Tyne, whom the 1891 census found at the house. Aged 67 and 66, they lived with their daughter Sarah, aged 30 (on the left?), and a 17-year old local girl, Anne Willis, as a domestic servant.

39

The Ratcliffe family – Samuel, Mary, their daughter Florence and baby son Charles – photographed outside their house, Little Beeleigh Farm, near Maldon, probably in the autumn of 1870. Mary's bunched hair and heavily trimmed dress put her up to the mark in fashion; Samuel's loose, un-coordinated look is perhaps more 'sixties'. Although an exposure time of as much as 20 seconds has given the sitters a certain stiffness, and slightly blurred their features, this remains an unusually intimate and charming study.

A much-photographed scene in Felsted, with the fifteenth-century guild hall in the centre, and the tower of the Church of Holy Cross behind. Spalding's main interest probably lay in the picture postcard market, opened by new postal regulations in 1894, but this is a somewhat earlier view. The guild hall had an interesting career, being used for about 3 centuries from 1564 as the schoolroom of Lord Rich's educational foundation. Inadequate for mid nineteenth-century needs, it was then sold off, and replaced by the present neo-Gothic range, designed by Fred Chancellor. The old building was used for various purposes – including, appropriately, a Sunday School – until the Old Felstedians bought it back out of sentiment in 1923.

The explosive growth in cycling in the late nineteenth century gave Essex villagers a new outside source of income – tapped here by the Cyclists Rest in Hatfield Peverel High Street, photographed in the early 1900s. Although the street is occupied only by a solitary waggon, a similar opportunity would soon be given by motorized traffic. Twenty years after this was taken, Hatfield Peverel boasted 3 'motor engineers', at least 2 of whom were cycle agents converted to the new cause.

In July 1891, the 4th Annual Archaeological and Botanical Ramble of the Chelmsford Odde Volumes took them on a tour of Blackmore, Greenstead and Ongar, stopping for tea and a photograph at Jericho (otherwise Blackmore Priory), legendary haunt of Henry VIII. Jericho, and a good deal of land in the parish, had been acquired in the 1880s by Thomas Hull (from Dorset via London), whom a census-taker in 1891 described as 'licensed victualler and farmer'. On this occasion, however, there was only tea: the urn can just be seen beside the right hand ground floor window.

A visit to St. Mary's church, Runwell, by 2 unidentified ladies, placed by their costume in about the 1870s. Many early photographs of churches are given particular interest by the drastic restorations undertaken by Victorian clerics. In this case, it was an Edwardian rector, Henry Harris, who in 1907–8 would partly rebuild the church and strip off the plaster seen here to reveal the stone beneath – and also a squint hole just to the right of the porch, which he promptly blocked up again. Harris's zeal for improvement even ran to his personally wiring the church and rectory for electric light in 1896.

This view of Stock, issued as a postcard, shows the High Street, looking north-east, with the Congregational Church of 1889 on the right. Mr. Parnell, who stands on the left in his butcher's apron, first appears in directories in 1899, and the photograph was probably taken at about that date. The gentleman on the right in the wide-brimmed hat has also found his way into the photograph of the village green on the opposite page.

Ingatestone High Street, looking towards Chelmsford, in about 1875. On the left, young George Camp (presumably) looks out from his shoemaker's shop to share the novel experience of being photographed. To the right lies the Ship Inn, run by Daniel Dennis, one of a dynasty of bricklayer-publicans. Only shortly afterwards, the shoemaker was Lucy Camp, already a widow in her thirties, with 5 young children and a lodger, and the Ship was in the hands of old Catherine Dennis, her soon-to-be-publican son apparently still laying bricks. The Ship's licence was later taken up by Henry King, a wheelwright, and finally surrendered in the early twentieth century, leaving of the inn only 'the repute of being rather damp, having a well under one of its floors'.

The Street at Roxwell, looking east, with the Chequers Inn half-hidden behind a screen of young trees. The mount of this photograph shows Spalding's address as 3 Tindal Square, so it was probably taken before his move to the High Street in the early 1890s. On the other hand, one can just make out a telegraph pole down the street on the left, outside Knight's bakery-cum-Post Office: in 1886 the nearest telegraph office had been at Writtle. Confirmation of the date as about 1890 is given by the tiny sign on the weatherboarded house in the foreground. It reads 'County Police'. Sure enough, the 1891 census reveals the residents as P.C. John Gentry, his wife Eliza, and their young family, including daughters Maud (aged 8) and Eliza (aged 5). Is it they who are watching from the gate?

Clean and abundant water was one of the greatest needs of the growing towns of Victorian England. Rochford was a case in point. In 1893 it was reported that the inhabitants were 'dependent upon two pumps, one of which is said not to contain wholesome water; while the other gives only a limited and totally inadequate yield, with the result that it is kept locked except for an hour every morning and an hour every evening, when the precious fluid is doled out at a half-penny a pail, each householder being allowed to purchase two buckets-full a day'. This pump in the market place was finally removed in 1902, when mains were laid from a new deep well at South Benfleet.

Along Stock High Street from the Congregational Church is an open green, with the village Post Office on the left (marked by a telegraph pole). On one example of the postcard made from this print – another is postmarked 1904 – an early collector has written 'prettier than it appears'. Stock certainly kept in use until very late the charming but not very practical pump seen here. In 1901 the County Medical Officer of Health reported 3 pumps in the village – one providing 'very impure water', the Jubilee pump 'much better water', and the well on the village green 'water of doubtful purity'. 'A public supply,' he thought, 'is much wanted here'.

Dunmow High Street, in its unreformed state at about the turn of the century: this view was in circulation as a postcard by 1902. The dusty road surface must have needed frequent visits by the water cart in summer, and Dunmow's water itself came from shallow wells. By 1908 it was the only town in the county still to lack a public water supply. A new borehole was then sunk into the chalk, and by 1916 the whole town had mains water; the redundant pump survives as a monument. At about the same time, the pavement was laid with flagstones and given kerbs, finally dividing this street into one space for vehicles and another for pedestrians.

The Angel Inn at Broomfield, run in the early twentieth century by Alfred Kime, formerly butler to the Wells family (the Angel was a Wells & Perry house), latterly publican and chairman of Broomfield Parish Council. The absence of motor traffic, and the heavy farm cart in the background, supply an atmosphere of timeless rural calm. In fact the Angel, a fifteenth-century building, had changed considerably over its history, and was to change even more. A later photograph by Spalding, probably of the 1930s, shows one chimney less, one dormer window more, a new window in the angle of the ground floor, and the fine saloon bar doorway moved some yards to the left. Later still, the gable end was pargetted – a nod to the dying age of rural craftsmanship.

The quay at Burnham-on-Crouch in about 1930: the Anchor Hotel still exists today, but this view has now been partly cut off by the raising of the sea wall. As so often in Spalding's pictures of old Essex, some things are not as old as they seem. A decade before this photograph was taken, the Anchor had no dormer window, but the nearest 2 bays of the front did have exposed weatherboarding. It seems that the nearer doorway may in fact have opened into a quite separate house: the census-taker of 1891 put the Anchor second on his schedule for the quay, reserving first place for the household of Andrew Rome, inspector of police.

'The retirement of Bradwell, its absolute freedom from bustle, or fashion, or excursion parties, are pleasing and most restful.' Thus a holiday-maker in 1897, rejoicing in the village's freedom from 'the grasp of the railway'. The isolation of the far tip of the Dengie peninsula certainly contributed to the peace of Bradwell's High Street, seen here in about 1905. The horse still ruled this road: the King's Head Hotel is advertising 'wagonette, pony & trap to let', and even a few years later another licensee combined hotel-keeping with saddlery.

Chipping Hill, Witham, in the early 1900s, with the White Horse Inn to the right. Beyond gapes the entrance to Mr. Quy the blacksmith's, the exposed inner sides of the door serving as a local noticeboard. This building is still a smithy today, although horses are no longer shod here. The small green in the background marks the site of the market place ('cheaping') which gave the settlement its name, and whose replacement by another on the main Colchester road to the south probably preserved this idyllic scene. Like many views of this type, Spalding had it printed as a postcard, the printing being done at Trier in the Rhineland.

A view across the Wear Pond on Writtle Green in the early 1900s, perhaps justifying the view of a vicar of the time, that a wayfarer coming upon the green with 'its weeping willows and its lime trees, its ancient houses with their uneven roofs . . . cannot but stop and consider that for those who dwell around it, "the lot has fallen in a fair ground!"'. And all within 2 miles of the county town. However, the garden on the right was not to be a garden for long: in December 1908, Lady Gooch from Hylands House opened a new brick-built village hall on the site.

Woodham Ferrers in about 1905, with the Post & Telegraph Office on the right, beyond the Bell Inn. Before the arrival in 1889 of the Maldon and Southminster branch of the Great Eastern, the village had been typical of isolated, depressed rural Essex, its population falling by nearly a third between 1851 and 1881. A modest revival was now underway, although the mid nineteenth-century peak of nearly 1000 souls had yet to be reached again when this view was taken.

These 2 photographs show Spalding far from his usual range, in King Street and Market Square at Saffron Walden. Both were issued among a set of postcards of the town, and probably taken with that in mind. The concurrence in King Street of Hardwick's fish shop on the left and Spurge's ('late Loomes') drapers on the right suggests a date of about 1905. The tall King Street Post Office, with the postmaster's flat jutting out on the first floor, was built in 1889, and in use until 1919. When this view was taken, it was open from 7 a.m. to 9 p.m., and 8 a.m. to 10 a.m. on Sundays. The square, unpaved, still has the peaceful air of a country market place, dominated by the Corn Exchange of 1850. This is perhaps deceptive: the waggon on the far side carries the words 'Great Eastern Railway Company'.

Two boys, two watering cans, and two churches: St. Andrew & All Saints, Willingale Spain, nearer the camera, and St. Christopher, Willingale Doe, beyond. The parish boundary runs across the road, just this side of the Bell Inn. Beyond it, against the churchyard wall, can be seen the village pump, where perhaps the watering cans have just been filled. There are several Spalding postcards of this spot, dating from the early 1900s, but this particular plate seems not to have been issued in postcard form.

A slightly contrived rural scene at East Hanningfield, which has been measured up for use as a postcard. The letters 'H.P.' are clearly visible on the barrow, but who this might indicate is not known. Perhaps Henry Picking of Botley House?

The Suffolk border received an unaccustomed visitor when Spalding took this photograph outside St. Andrew's church, Wormingford. The parish had a population in 1901 of 380, and over half of them must be here. Exactly why is not known, although styles of dress place the picture in the first years of the twentieth century, and the flowering horse-chestnut reveals the time of year. One possibility would be Empire Day, 24 May, which was celebrated after 1902 as a reminder of the colonies' help to Britain in the Boer War. The Union Jack was central to the event, and a companion picture shows the crowd peering up to the flag on the church tower.

The Big House

Felix Hall

Felix Hall, Kelvedon, built in about 1715, was the family home of the
Westerns. In the late nineteenth century it was occupied by a series of
tenants before the estate – and apparently the furniture too – was sold off
in 1913, leaving the house and a small park for a daughter of the family
and her husband, a member of a City shipping and insurance firm. Sold on

3 more times, the hall was partly demolished in 1939, and the remainder
largely destroyed by fire in 1940. These photographs show the splendid
drawing room, with its Italian marble chimneypiece; the garden front; and
the hall's main elevation, with a gathering of the East Essex Hunt.

"Felix Hall"

Easton Lodge

Easton Lodge at Little Easton stood at the centre of the late Victorian social whirl. Its owner, Frances Countess of Warwick, became famous for her lavish hospitality and her intimacy with Edward Prince of Wales. These photographs show – right – the Lodge with its famous gardens (the Tudor is mostly mock, the result of a rebuilding in 1847); one of the glittering reception rooms; and a formal group which Spalding was summoned by telegram to take during a house party in 1891. The Prince – just short of his 50th birthday – stands in the centre in a brown felt hat and check ulster; his hostess is on his left; and on her left is the future Queen Mary. Other members of the party can be identified from Spalding's own key.

The Countess's later years – she died only in 1938 – shook the poise of this photograph. Her income was undermined by extravagance and agricultural depression, and her social position by her increasingly utopian politics. Easton Lodge itself was badly damaged by fire in 1918, and what remained was demolished in 1947.

1. H.R.H. the Prince of Wales; 2. H.R.H. the Duchess of York;
3. H.S.H. the Duchess of Teck; 4. H.S.H. Prince Francis of Teck;
5. The Countess of Warwick; 6. The Earl of Warwick;
7. Lady Eva Greville; 8. Lord Gordon Lennox;
9. Lady Lister Kaye; 10. Lady Lillian Wemyss;
11. Count Soveral; 12. Count Mensdorff

Hylands House

Hylands House at Widford, seen here from front and back, has had a chequered past. It was built in about 1730 for Sir John Comyns, a successful Essex lawyer, as a red brick house of 2 storeys, only 7 bays wide. In the late eighteenth and early nineteenth centuries it was owned successively, and considerably altered, by a Danish West Indian merchant and a Dutch-born banker, who by 1818 had created an elegant neo-classical mansion of 2 storeys, with low side-wings. In 1839, it was bought by John Attwood, a wealthy ironmaster and future bankrupt, who by 1848 had greatly enlarged and remodelled the house. This, its final form as a private home, was what Spalding photographed. In his time, the house continued to provided landed respectability to various owners of industrial wealth: Arthur Pryor (1858–c.1905), a partner in Truman, Hanbury, Buxton & Co., brewers; Sir Daniel Gooch Bt. (c.1905–1920), grandson of a chairman of the Great Western Railway; and finally, after a brief interval, John Mackenzie Hanbury – another brewer – and his widow Christine. After her death the now decaying Hylands was bought in 1966 by Chelmsford Borough Council. Demolition of Attwood's additions has brought its external appearance back to that of the early nineteenth century, but discussions on its future continue.

Members of the servants' hall at Hylands, photographed at the back of the house. Not easily dated, but the elaborate blouses with peaked shoulders worn by some of the maids would have been fashionable with their mistresses in about 1890, when Hylands was owned by the brewer Arthur Pryor. The 1891 census does indeed show an indoors establishment of 16, although unfortunately made up of 3 men and 13 women. It also, incidentally, shows how few personal links might exist between the big house and its surroundings. Of the entire household, family included, of 24 people, only 2 – Arthur Pryor's little grandson John and laundrymaid Lucy Blanks – had been born in Essex. Among the servants, the central trio of butler, housekeeper and cook came from Worcestershire, Lincolnshire and Westmoreland.

Some unidentified members of the Gooch family of Hylands, the more fashion-conscious displaying the tight waists, full upper sleeves, elaborate hats, and delight in decoration typical of the Edwardian period.

Lord Kitchener of Khartoum, Secretary of State for War, leaves Hylands House in August 1915 after conducting an inspection of troops in the park. This was Kitchener's first and last visit to Chelmsford: less than a year later he was to be lost in the sinking of H.M.S. Hampshire. By the time of his visit, Sir Daniel Gooch had converted part of the house into a military hospital.

Happier times at Hylands in August 1920, as Sir Daniel Gooch's eldest daughter Phyllis and her husband Frank Parrish leave for their honeymoon, in a cream Crossley tourer acquired a few days before. The military hospital had been demobbed early in 1919, and for a moment a breath of the Roaring Twenties touched the house. However, Sir Daniel's eldest son had died while serving with the Navy in 1915, and only a month after the wedding he put the estate up for sale, himself moving down to Hampshire until his death in 1926.

Skreens Park

Skreens Park, Roxwell, was home to the Bramston family for 2 centuries, but the last of the line let it to a series of tenants, and finally sold in about 1908 to a Cheshire gentleman, William Shaw. Thus opened the last, most gorgeous and shortest phase of the house's history. By the time of his death 2 years later, Shaw had greatly enlarged the building, and stuffed it with trophies of every kind. Modern conveniences abounded – there were no less than 4 bathrooms, and a private electricity plant driven by a 100-volt Crompton dynamo – but most striking are the lush interiors, furnished in the Imperial-Jacobean style at its most splendid. Notice on the hall table (bottom right) the carefully arranged group of mechanical toys – including an early gramophone – and the central framed photograph, presumably of Shaw himself. Yet in 1914 Shaw's son put the estate up for sale, and by 1921 the house had been razed.

Danbury Palace

The obscure origins of Fred Spalding senior do admit one firm statement, that he was born in Danbury. This may help to explain why one of his earliest surviving photographs – above right – is of Bishop George Murray of Rochester, who died in 1860. Among the bishop's other distinctions (he was a nephew of the Duke of Atholl, and his great-grandfather and namesake fought for Bonnie Prince Charlie) he was the first episcopal resident of Danbury Palace, a neo-Tudor pile bought for the bishops of

Rochester in 1845, when they were given responsibility for Essex.

Below is a view of the palace itself. Above left, in his remarkable 3-wheeler, is Bishop Thomas Claughton, who died there in 1892. The house afterwards passed back into private hands, and is now (1992) a management training centre.

Bishop Thomas Claughton and his household at the rear of Danbury Palace

Stisted Hall

At Stisted Hall in June 1900, James Paxman entertained almost the whole village in celebration of the British victories in South Africa. Spalding captured them at tea in front of the hall, under portraits of Queen Victoria and Baden-Powell, the defender of Mafeking. The 'Essex County Standard' noted that all the tables were 'decorated with choice plants, the pots of which were encircled with the national colours, red, white and blue'. Every guest was given a small Union Jack, bearing the single word 'Pretoria', the centre of Boer resistance. This photograph seems a perfect image of a stable, rural community – falsely, since Paxman, founder of the Colchester engineering firm, was squire for barely a decade. He bought in for £40,000 in 1894, and sold out in 1907.

Victorian ingenuity in the use of glass, wood and iron created one of the most distinctive features of the country house – the conservatory, combining delicate engineering with the exotic plants collected or improved by the intrepid explorers and nurserymen of the time. Here is an example from Stisted Hall, demonstrating the later nineteenth-century trend away from formal planting towards more 'natural' masses of flowers and foliage.

The famous pleasure grounds at Hylands included this greenhouse – later converted into an indoor swimming pool, and demolished in 1966.

The 'big house' usually stands alone in these photographs, its means of support – the estate and the estate workers – invisible behind an imposing facade. Here, to end, is an exception. Faulkbourne Hall in August 1907 saw lavish celebrations for the coming of age of the eldest son, John Oxley Parker, who was just down from Oxford. Social distinctions were nicely observed. There was a garden party; then a lunch for the estate's tenants, not only from Faulkbourne but also from Woodham Mortimer, Purleigh, Bradwell, and even Bermondsey; and finally tea on the lawn for the cottagers of Faulkbourne and Woodham Mortimer. It must have been then that Spalding took this snapshot of Edwardian rural society. Even the local bobby was there . . .

The Pursuit of Pleasure

An Edwardian afternoon tea is served on the lawn at Stonedene, Ingatestone. The contrast between the man's relatively informal attire, with his white tennis shoes, and the women's elaborately structured clothes, mirrors the nature of the event: a preserve of the leisured classes, but tightly fenced with convention.

This comfortable scene, from the late 1880s, took place at the Gate House, Ingatestone, newly built for himself and his young family by the architect George Sherrin (1843–1909). London-born, and by this time with a London practice, he had long served in Fred Chancellor's office in Chelmsford, and some of his best work lies – or lay – in Essex. The discreetly antique elevations of the Gate House make it the more surprising that he also designed the Kursaal at Southend. On the croquet lawn here are his wife Ellen (seated furthest right, she was the daughter of a Chelmsford organ builder) and daughters Dorothy (with the mallet), Kate and Barbara (the baby). Mr. Crozier, the gardener, is still busy laying out the house's notable gardens.

More demanding recreation was available from this Dennis travelling library van, able to hold 3,000 books, which Essex County Council acquired in 1930. At the time, the county ran only 7 branch libraries, but there were 170 local centres – marked with plaques like the one visible here – where books could be chosen by local people and left for a period before collection. In its first 9 months, the van delivered over 45,000 books. It should perhaps be said that

Spalding had his doubts about public libraries. Many years before, in 1904, when Chelmsford Borough Council decided to build a Science and Art School, Library and Museum in what is now Victoria Road South, he spoke 'in favour of the Art School but was opposed to the Free Library. He said the rates of Chelmsford were rising by leaps and bounds, and, as everyone knew, trade was bad'.

One of the features of Chelmsford's inter-war Hospital Carnivals was fancy dress. Local firms and organizations competed vigorously with decorated floats, but here are 2 shots of the children's event. The little schoolmaster is from 1934. The date of the elderly young gentleman is not known, but he must be from 1931 or later, for the hospital contributory scheme began in January of that year, and by December had 10,300 members. It was a vital element in the finances of a hospital which was rapidly expanding to meet the district's needs: in 1930, one third of expenditure came directly from payments by patients.

Few of Fred Spalding's portraits escape the stiffness of the studio pose, but here he managed to capture the lively curiosity of his subjects. The occasion is unknown, but we seem to be at a fair in the 1930s – perhaps one of the regular events on King's Head Meadow in Chelmsford?

The mayoral procession lines up in the New London Road, Chelmsford, for the 1930 Hospital Carnival: the Chelmsford & Essex Hospital lies behind the trees to the right. As a young man Spalding had been commissioned in 1883 to photograph the original hospital buildings. As Mayor of Chelmsford, he had presided over the first Carnival in 1923. In 1930, as usual, he was chairman of the Carnival Committee, but this photograph was actually taken for J. W. Austin, the local Ford dealer, who supplied these cars for the Mayor and Corporation.

Messing about in and on the water was a favourite Victorian pastime, and one with many photographic possibilities . . .

A bargeful of Chelmsford Odde Volumes, members of a society set up in 1888 'to encourage archaeology, science, literature, music and the fine arts'. This task they pursued with unflinching jocularity. The occasion here is their 'summer ramble' of July 1899 in 'the good ship 'Nancy Bell', bound from the Port of Chelmers-ford on a Voyage of Discovery and Research in the (comparatively) Unknown and perilous Waters which lie between Moulsham and the distant shores of the Blackwater' [the parody is of H.M.S. Challenger, not the U.S.S. Enterprise]. Oddly, Spalding did not belong, but the crew included many influential members of local society, including Fred Chancellor the architect; Robert Cook, moving spirit of the County Cycling & Athletic Association; J. H. Nicholas, secretary of the Essex Education Committee ('second mate'); and Dr. John Thresh, County Medical Officer of Health and unrivalled expert on local water supplies.

Boating on the lake at Danbury Palace: a view marked up for use as a postcard

A lone oarsman at Pitt Place, Great Baddow. The carefully timed exposure of this plate has left the boat and its reflection sharply defined, while giving a softness to the breeze-blown trees.

Below, and on the facing page, are the more public pleasures of Chelmsford's recreation ground. Laid out beside the River Can in 1894, it embodied the belief that a growing town needed public open space, just as it needed roads or sewers. A long list of subscriptions was headed by £500 from Henry Collings Wells, Chelmsford's county councillor, and ran down to include 12 seats donated by a working men's committee, and a group of swans given by Mr. E. H. Carter – perhaps the birds pictured above right. At the opening ceremony, Mrs. Wells, the Mayoress and the Deputy Mayoress were presented with commemorative albums of Fred Spalding's photographs. He himself attended as a young borough councillor, and later sat down to a public lunch, the catering being entrusted to his brother Arthur, of the Rayleigh Arms.

Sporting Lives

The Falcon Bowling Club was formed in 1908, and its green laid out on the former garden of the Bell Inn, Tindal Street, in 1909. The ladies' cornucopian hats place this photograph not long afterwards. Edwardian headgear was a topic of interest even to Edwardians: when the Essex Education Committee in 1907 decided not to include millinery on the elementary school curriculum, a relieved local journalist commented that 'there are more useful branches of knowledge for girls to acquire than the ability to arrange artificial flowers and dead birds on a hat'.

A group photograph, probably taken at the swimming gala held in June 1907, in aid of hospital funds. The Chelmsford Swimming Club, in the open-air pool built the previous year, beat their guests from Colchester at water polo and in a team race, before entertaining them to a 'meat tea'. Among the participants in the diving display was a Spalding — perhaps Fred's young son Wilfred (born in 1893). At the club's second annual sports in August, he won a heat of the 100 yards handicap, and triumphed in object diving. In the same year, the Borough Council voted to provide swimming lessons at the pool for the children in its schools.

With the introduction, in the mid-1880s, of rear-wheel drive, and then of pneumatic tyres, cycling became ever more popular. For women especially it provided an activity both athletic and respectable. This photograph of the Chelmer Cycling Club on Springfield Green in about 1897–9 certainly exudes the latter quality. With motor cars still few, expensive and unreliable, the prospects for two-wheeled travel seemed endless. In 1893,

Robert Cook, secretary to the county association, had written breathlessly that 'great as cycling is, it is but a little beyond its infancy, but there is no fear of its being cut out till we have the long-looked-for flying machine'. In 1892, there were 27 cycling clubs in the county, with 1,355 members all told.

The strain shows at an Edwardian tug-of-war – not identified, but perhaps at a County Show. An ancient sport, the tug-of-war was re-invented by Victorian athletes in the 1870s (allegedly at the Woolwich Garrison Sports in 1874), and became highly popular, finally achieving recognition from the Essex County Cycling & Athletic Association in 1927.

The burning question   WHO'S ASHES?

Cricket was one of Fred Spalding's great enthusiasms. Here it finds free rein in his window. The picture carries no date, but it is tempting to ascribe it to the shop window competition organized in May 1934 to mark the visit of the Australian team to Chelmsford, after the controversial test matches of 1932–3. Although they had previously met Essex at the Leyton ground, the Australians had not been to Chelmsford before, and this match was the highlight of the Cricket Festival Week (chairman of the organizing committee, F. Spalding).

A sweltering July Saturday in 1901 saw the 20th annual race meeting of the Essex County Cycling & Athletic Association, held on the old cricket ground in New Street, Chelmsford. The Great Eastern ran special trains from London and Colchester, the town's shops closed for the afternoon, bands played, and the lucky winners were presented with prizes by the Lady Mayoress of London (a late stand-in for the Countess of Warwick). The novelty event of the day was a cycle polo match, won by Walthamstow Town. The new maltings in the background are a reminder of the ultimately industrial fate of this site, covered by Marconi's new factory in 1912.

The Essex Union Hunt meets in March 1892 at Baddow Lodge, Great Baddow, where James Tabor entertained them to breakfast. According to the 'Essex Weekly News', 'Mr. F. Spalding, of Chelmsford, secured some successful photos of the picturesquely grouped hounds and huntsmen', before the hunt went off to find its fox near Galleywood Common. Baddow Lodge itself was demolished in the 1930s: only Tabor's Hill now recalls its location.

Ilford Quoits Club, the leading local team, probably photographed at the Essex County Association for Quoits cup final, on the ground beside the King's Head, Chelmsford High Street, on 9 September 1893. After an exciting finish, Ilford beat Chelmsford to retain the cup by 156 points to 150. Only a few weeks later, they defeated Custom House to win the All England Cup outright.

An Edwardian shooting party at Old Riffhams, Little Baddow

At School

The boys of Chelmsford Charity School, in their dark blue uniforms, photographed in 1862 with their master, Joseph Mitchell. The school had been set up by a group of subscribers in 1713, long before the days of public education, and taught about 50 children (originally poor children) from Chelmsford and Moulsham. Although rebuilt in 1861 on a site in Church Street, north of the churchyard, the school lost much of its purpose in 1870 with the introduction of universal elementary education, and in 1878 it closed.

Playtime at Woodham Ferrers Church of England School, built in 1846, and providing space for the education of 163 children (at 8 square feet per child). In the late nineteenth century, over 100 were regularly taught here, although attendance was rather seasonal. The master wrote feelingly in his log for October 1897: 'children are constantly being kept from school by their parents to roam the fields and roads in search of blackberries with as much unconcern as if there existed no law to compel children to attend school'. Other worries were the many young heads 'full of livestock', and the muddiness of the playground – the latter much in evidence here. Only once, in December 1901, did he note that 'the children of the school were photographed today': sadly, not this photograph.

The Essex Industrial School was founded in 1872 by J. Brittain Pash, the agricultural machinery manufacturer, and housed from 1877 in this building at Rainsford End, Chelmsford. A mainly practical education was provided for destitute and neglected boys, who, it was observed in 1900, 'strike a visitor as being a clean-living, well-mannered, fairly-treated set of English lads, who lead a healthy out-of-door life'. Here they can be seen tending the school strawberry bed and learning to sew. The institution, latterly known as the Essex Home School, closed in 1980, and its buildings were later demolished.

The Industrial School made a point of obtaining photographs of the boys in its care. Here is one from Spalding's studio of Henry Dyball, late of Windsor, who was detained in 1880, aged 9, 'not being under control'. The admission register notes that he could read 'words of 4 letters' and write 'a little'.

A display of swimming and diving by the boys of the Essex Industrial School, and – below – the school bazaar of June 1904, which raised £130 for new dormitories. Among the stall-holders was Fred's daughter Constance. The Mayor, George Taylor, was reported as stressing that 'it was not only a school for imparting general knowledge, but the lads were also taught many practical subjects which would be of very good service to them when they went out into the world'. Besides drill, there were demonstrations of boys 'busy at the wash-tub, in the carpenter's shop, in the needle room, the tailor's shop and the shoemaker's shop'.

A different type of education was provided by Felsted Grammar School. Founded in 1564 by Richard Lord Rich – a London lawyer who had made his name and fortune in the dissolution of the monasteries – as a free school for 80 Essex boys, in the second half of the nineteenth century it was re-established and rebuilt as a modern boarding school, supported in part by fees (£62 a year, at the turn of the century). Rifle drill was begun in 1859, and Felsted took part in the Ashburton Shield competition at Bisley from 1892. Here is one of its Bisley Eights (actually nine), from 1899. The rifles are apparently Lee-Enfields, as introduced to the British Army in 1895, although they show elements of the earlier Lee-Metford pattern.

Pupils of the tiny boarding school run by Miss Rosa Barker at Beadel's Hall, Chignal Smealey. In 1891, she – with 2 assistant mistresses, a cook and a housemaid – had 14 girls and boys under her care, aged from 4 to 14. Most came from nearby villages, but there were also 5 from London. An advertisement in 1907 boasted a curriculum of English, French, German, Music, Drawing, Dancing and Needlework – the traditional polite accomplishments. The needlework, at least, is much in evidence here . . .

The 1902 Education Act, allowing the new Local Education Authorities to provide secondary education, and a growing readiness to recognize and develop female talent, prompted the opening of Chelmsford County High School for Girls in 1907. Even the school buildings, designed by Fred Chancellor, Chelmsford's mayor, marked the change, having purpose-built chemistry and physics laboratories, although physical education for the time being had to take place in the assembly hall. The 'Essex Review', commenting that it was 'time that the claims of female education were recognized', noted that 'especially is this important now when so colossal a share of the teaching of the nation's children falls, worthily, into the hands of women'.

Adult education in action at a County Council cookery class, probably in the 1930s. Even in the 1890s, the Technical Instruction Committee had tried in its local classes to spread proper principles of cookery, and to show that 'a varied diet is as cheap as a monotonous one, whilst it is far more nourishing and acceptable'. The same concerns led the council to print, between 1920 and 1939, no less than 387,000 copies of its 'Essex Cookery Book', full of simple, cheap recipes. Of this vast production, only a single copy of the 11th edition survives at the Record Office, but perhaps the rest are still, as its introduction hoped, adding 'to the health and happiness of the county of Essex'.

Farms, Factories and Salesmanship

When Arthur Young made his 'Six Weeks Tour' of Southern England and Wales in 1767, he was surprised to find that on Lord Clare's estate at Gosfield the draught animals were not horses but oxen – an innovation 'highly ridiculed by all the neighbouring farmers, who would as soon believe that an ox could speak as draw'. This photograph of Spalding's must be over a century later, but whether it was posed for his camera, or whether Lord Clare had local successors in his experiment, is not known. In any event, by the end of Spalding's life, the tractor was rapidly displacing muscle-power on the farm.

Most photographic portraits were made to order, but it was surely Spalding's own interest in the fading rural world which led him to this picture. Charles Sweeting (1826–1913) spent his working life around Broomfield, as one of the 'Ag. Labs.' beloved of Victorian census-takers. A real countryman, but the photograph is quite studied. The laying out for inspection of Mr. Sweeting's tools, his 'elevens' of bread and cheese, and of himself, all speak of the student behind the lens, recording a piece of social history.

The might of the agricultural machinery industry on display at an Essex Show of the early 1900s – perhaps the Jubilee Show held at Chelmsford in 1907, at which Spalding himself put on 'a picturesque show of portraits, landscapes, animals, and architectural views'. The firms taking part here were at the cutting edge of innovation: Bentall's of Maldon even manufactured motor cars.

A traction engine at the Meeson family farm, Rettendon Place, being used to power a threshing box. Inside the box, a drum separated grain from husks, and a series of riddles removed the chaff, depositing the grain in sacks, while the straw was thrown from the rear of the box and gathered up by pitchfork.

Older methods of agriculture contribute to the charm of this view of the park at Castle Hedingham, one of a group taken before the estate was put up for sale in 1896. The twelfth-century keep was already on the tourist trail: a guide book of 1907 complains that 'the common folk . . . go to infinite pains to scrawl their names and addresses and the date of their important visit upon the walls, possibly to show the result of their Board School education'. An agricultural labourer would have had to spend about half his daily wage for a copy of this photograph, sold unmounted at 1s. 3d. (about 6p).

The corn trade, a central part of Chelmsford's economy, once took place in the lobby of the Shire Hall. This came to an end in 1858 with the building of the Corn Exchange, to designs by Fred Chancellor. Here is the Exchange in about 1905: shortly afterwards, Collins & Son moved their china shop down to the corner of the Springfield Road (see page 28), and the shop itself made way just after the First World War for the new London Joint City and Midland Bank. The Corn Exchange was demolished in 1969, and nothing now remains of this view except the Shire Hall to the right and the statue of Judge Nicholas Tindal, erected in 1851.

Trade in progress inside the Corn Exchange, sometime between the wars. This view reveals clearly its cast iron and glass construction, so reminiscent of a mid-Victorian railway station. The acoustics seem to have been rather along the same lines, but despite this the Exchange also acted as the town's main public hall, and Spalding himself was one of the leading impresarios. In February 1892, for example, the 'Essex Weekly News' ran a fulsome review of a 'Grand Evening Concert . . . by Mr. Edward Lloyd and his celebrated concert party', held in the Exchange through 'the enterprise of Mr. Fred Spalding, who . . . ran a heavy risk in retaining such tip-top talent'.

Springs and boreholes provided Chelmsford with a more-or-less inadequate water supply for many years, until in 1922 the Borough Council decided to take water from the River Chelmer too. In 1923 they acquired Sandford Mill – once a watermill, but converted to steam in 1870 – and in 1929 a new waterworks began operations on the site. This photograph shows the mill as it was in 1923. Below are workmen digging out reservoirs behind the old mill pond (the contractor was French's of Buckhurst Hill), and the new works, with the mill house still surviving on the right hand side.

Joshua Mallett's mill at Little Waltham in about 1860. The white posts in the foreground are thought to be tenter frames, relics of the cloth industry, on which fulled cloth was stretched ('on tenter hooks'). Behind, the new engine house marks a shift from water-power to steam, but it was not enough to save the mill, which closed at the turn of the century and was later demolished.

A different fate met the steam mill at East Hanningfield. The miller, George Castle, converted it to oil in the mid-1920s, but by 1937 he seems to have given up milling altogether, and is listed as a wireless engineer. The Austin van shown here, advertising Castle's Wireless Service, was registered in 1932.

A photograph of the Home Farm at Ingatestone Hall. Nothing here, from the Elizabethan brick barn with its pigeon loft in the porch, to the farmworkers' working clothes, allows one to say much more than 'late nineteenth century'. Timeless, however, this farmyard was not. The Petre estates, like most arable lands, underwent a profound depression from the 1870s. In 1893, Lord Petre's agent, after a dozen years during which rents had fallen by 43%, reported despairingly that 'some very strong measures

[tariffs against foreign grain] must be brought to bear . . . if the chief industry of this country is not to be stamped out'. The tenant of Home Farm had given notice to quit, unable to compete with the prevailing low prices. The crisis was worsened, the agent thought, by the Petres 'dealing in a liberal manner with the property', and spending heavily on repairs and improvements – a habit which has preserved this barn to the present day.

Budd's baker's shop stood at 11 Moulsham Street, Chelmsford, just south of the junction with Baddow Road. Reflected in its upper windows here is J. G. Bond's furniture store, occupying the old militia armoury on the opposite side of the street. The photograph was taken around 1930, when Budd's made daily deliveries to the villages roundabout; the second shot

shows their van on the edge of its range at Galleywood. It also visited Boreham, Widford, Great Baddow and Writtle. The van's trim appearance was a matter of pride: in 1929, Budd's won 1st prize in the 'best turn-out, light vanner' class at the Chelmsford Hospital Carnival.

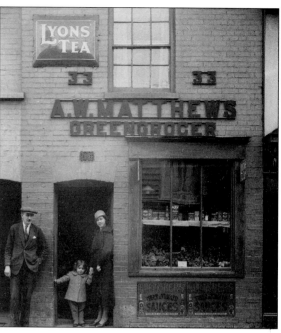

...pple-packing in progress at W. Seabrook & Sons, of Springfield and Boreham. William *eabrook, a Boreham native who founded the firm in 1887, was an apostle of modern methods, ...mplaining that 'no class is so conservative as fruit growers, unless it be farmers'. Seabrook ...lieved that 'just so soon as the English grower standardized, packed and graded properly, and ...t on the market fruit as reliable as that which came from abroad, then, and then only would ...at produce take its proper place'. Such ideas, seen here being put into practice, came to wider ...uition in 1928 with the introduction of the National Mark for apples and pears, and in the ...llowing year with the first of a series of Essex Fruit Shows in Chelmsford's Corn Exchange, ...uly photographed by Spalding for the 'Essex Farmers' Journal'.

... and perhaps a less up-to-date sector of the fruit and vegetable trade, in Moulsham Street, Chelmsford. Despite the need to supplement greengrocery with tea, Oxo and other dry goods – or perhaps as a result – this business survived in the same family into the 1950s.

A magnificent and gory display at Hugh Wright's butcher's shop in Springfield Road, Chelmsford, 2 weeks before Christmas in 1923. The prize-winning carcasses, and Spalding's services, were no doubt both acquired with a view to promoting trade. In the doorway stand Miss Wright and John Perriment; peeping from an upper window, unwilling to be excluded from such an occasion, is John's sister-in-law. Hugh Wright, a Rutland man who had made his career in Co-operative butchery before acting as Chief Meat Agent in the First World War, had set up in Chelmsford only in 1920, but in 1925 was chosen mayor in succession to Spalding.

A slightly burlesque, but informative view of Jackson's dairy farm at Wickford. The early twentieth century saw a new emphasis on non-arable farming, with improvements in yield, quality and marketing, and milk was a key area. Proposals to establish local milk record societies were made in 1914, and in 1928 Woolshots came fifth in a county competition for best-kept milk records, Jackson's cowman G. Hazell winning a special prize of £1 for the best records 'kept by a cowman or person actually engaged in milking'. New rules of hygiene had their effect in these cowmen's clothing: in 1920, Essex had become the first county to hold a clean milk competition. The Milk Marketing Board arrived in 1933, but this photograph – probably of the early twenties – shows that some farmers were already well aware of the power of the positive image.

The Co-Op, with 3 million members by 1914, was one of the first national grocery chains, catering to the mass market of urban Britain. Their stand in Chelmsford's Corn Exchange is promoting one of the new era's typical products, patented in the U.S.A. in 1873, and rather carefully defined by Parliament in 1887 as 'all substances, whether compounds or otherwise, prepared in imitation of butter and whether mixed with butter or not'. Ramparts of suet ('Sutox Puts Life Into Your Puddings') vividly recall a time when fat was not bad for you. Ranks of mincemeat jars, and the crowning Christmas cracker, reveal the month of this photograph, but the year is unknown.

Shop windows were often decorated in competition between traders, but this example seems to be a purely commercial venture. On 18 March 1932, the 'Essex Chronicle' carried on its front page the exhortation 'See the Painting Demonstration in the window of Hasler & Hance (H. & S. Hance), Tindal Street, Chelmsford from 8 a.m. to 6 p.m., by the Robbialac Family. Dry Distemper (in all colours) 1/6 3^1/$_2$ lbs. . . . Hard Gloss Paint 1/6, 2/9, 5/3 per tin. Grate Enamel, 6d. tin . . .'. It comes as a slight shock to recognize that even in the 1930s family values were being used to sell ironmongery.

A tempting display by Cramphorn Ltd. at a caged bird show in Chelmsford's Corn Exchange, sometime between the wars (the Chelmsford & District Cage Bird Society held its first show – not at the Exchange – in 1928). The founder of the firm, corn merchant Thomas Cramphorn (1845–1912), had been an alderman and 6 times Mayor of Chelmsford, a near neighbour of Spalding in the High Street, and a fellow member of the Springfield Lodge of Freemasons, so there may have been sentimental as well as commercial reasons for taking this photograph.

The best advertising slogans never date, and it is unlucky for dating purposes that Henry J. Heinz invented the '57 Varieties' in New York as long ago as 1896. However, the company's great expansion in Britain took place between the wars, its canned soups being manufactured here from 1930. The power of the international brand name is well-illustrated by this window at 76 High Street, Chelmsford, of Luckin Smith, wholesale and family grocers. Originating in the 1880s, with Fred Luckin Smith and his family living over the shop, by the early 1930s this firm had 4 other sets of premises in Chelmsford, and 11 branches elsewhere in east Essex. No doubt it was very familiar to Fred Spalding: in 1907, when he was vice-president of the 87-strong Chelmsford Traders Association, Luckin Smith was its treasurer.

The traditions of rural industry lived into the 1860s with Messrs. Hills, Shonk and Isabel, 3 employees of Wells & Perry's brewery in Duke Street, Chelmsford. Their elaborate smocks, and Isabel's fustian jacket, strike a dissonant note with the photographer's stock classical backdrop, borrowed from traditional portraiture. The brewery itself was taken over by Taylor Walker & Co. in 1934 and demolished for the sake of its valuable town centre site, beer for the company's pubs being brought from London instead.

The staff of the Writtle Brewery, sometime in the late nineteenth century; the brewer, Joseph Hardcastle, was also a Liberal M.P.. The tools and products of the various tradesmen here – cooper, wheelwright, bricklayer, drayman – are reminders that breweries were among the first large businesses to cover the whole span from production through to retail sale. In the 1860s, Writtle served pubs not only in Chelmsford but also as far as Witham, North Weald and Brentwood. Breweries were also early takeover targets: Writtle was absorbed by a Gravesend firm in 1902, and closed down in the 1920s.

The corn trade and the beer trade were closely linked. Ridleys, now one of the last remaining independent local brewers, took early advantage of steam power and rail transport with their Townfield Mill, built before 1848 beside the tracks at Chelmsford. But the mill had an unlucky history, apparently being burned down in 1860, 1869 and – for the third and final time – 1969.

Sun Street, Billericay, between about 1900 and 1910. The Rising Sun had once been a coaching inn, and in 1898 could still be described by an auctioneer as 'situate in a most exceptionable position . . . on the main road from London to Southend where all the carriage and bicycle traffic must pass'. With stabling for 8 horses at the back, it was an ideal spot for the 2 Brentwood vets, Sydney Vincent and Richard Philp, to set up their branch practice (Mondays and Fridays only). The dray, making a delivery from Ind Coope's brewery in Romford, is another reminder of the already close links between these towns of south-east Essex.

Towards the end of Spalding's career, the growth in motor traffic, and corresponding spread of arterial roads, brought a new phenomenon in pubs: the road house. With the construction of Chelmsford's first bypass (Princes Road and Chelmer Road) in 1932, the Army & Navy in the Baddow Road was rebuilt on a new site and on a grand scale, to catch trade passing the new junction. Here is a view of the old pub taken – to judge by the bus timetable on its wall – after 30 June 1930, when Eastern National ran its first services. Very much altered, this building still survives, to the south of the present roundabout.

. . . and here is the new road house, in the style sometimes known dismissively as Brewer's Tudor. Advertised as 'a superb Temple of Bacchus', or, more accurately, 'a different kind of inn', one of its advantages was the ability to serve non-alcoholic drinks and light refreshments away from the traditional bar. A new type of traveller demanded a new type of service, and the buildings needed to deliver it.

The Windmill Inn at South Hanningfield – with a brewer's dray from Wells & Perry of Chelmsford edging out of the picture on the left. The clarity of the dry gelatin plate allows us to read the names of the licensee, T[homas] Hunt, and of [Herbert] Markham, the Springfield carrier whose cart stands on the left, piled with boxes. Together, they date the photograph to between 1900 and 1914.

At the White Horse, Widford, on the main road from London, the 2 Spaldings recorded 2 eras in the licensed trade. To the left is a view by Frederick senior, recopied by his son from a cracked and dirty plate. The clothing styles – high stovepipe hats for the men, a wide crinoline for the lady of the house, Ann Thorn – suggest a date of about 1860. To the right

is a view of the same house rebuilt, taken between 1927 and 1935. In the 1850s George Thorn, a tenant of the Hylands estate, had had a brewhouse, dairy, butcher's shop, piggeries and granary. In the 1920s the White Horse was simply an inn, and Ind Coope's tenant simply an innkeeper.

At the Old Bell Inn, Woodham Walter, the Chelmsford Brewery took a different approach. The Tudor building had changed gradually over the centuries: the single storey to the right is a nineteenth-century extension. In 1930, however, it underwent drastic restoration. The plaster was stripped off, to produce the black-and-white effect then fashionable; a porch

was added; and modern leaded lights replaced the existing windows. A feature on the changes in the 'Essex Chronicle' reported that Woodham Walter 'remains the quiet peaceful village of the days gone by, and the Old Bell is in keeping with the surroundings'. In taking these 2 pictures, Spalding showed a piece of heritage under construction.

Brickmaking at Messrs. Beach & Sons, Rainsford End, Chelmsford. Growing demand and easier transport by rail had led the industry to expand beyond its traditional locations in south Essex, but labour relations were not always sunny. In April 1914, in the midst of the wave of agricultural and industrial unrest which preceded the First World War, Beach's brickmakers struck for a threepenny increase in their pay of 4s.8d. (about 23p) for every 1,000 bricks made. It is not known whether they won or lost.

In the 1920s, the traction engine was nearing the end of its 30-year reign in rural England, but it was still a steam tractor, built by Garrett's of Leiston, Suffolk, in 1923, that provided hauling power for this huge oak, felled by Jack Playle of Heybridge. The plate is one of a series commissioned by the firm: others show the felling process (by axe, saw and human effort) and road haulage by a team of horses.

An earlier era in the timber trade, apparently in the yard of a willow merchant. In the early 1900s, demand for cricket bats was so great, and supply so limited, that the cricket bat willow became the most valuable tree grown in Britain. Essex was the centre of production.

Agricultural engineering in the workshops of J. Brittain Pash Ltd. at Chelmsford. The business was begun in 1866 on Joseph Pash's own farm at Galleywood, moving to successively larger premises in central Chelmsford, near the Corn Exchange and livestock market. This is probably Market Buildings, built in 1892 on the old Grammar School playing field, and demolished to make way for the newest extension to County Hall. As late as 1930, Spalding wrote that Chelmsford 'has always been and I hope will always remain an agricultural town, for we as traders have to thank the farmers for the hearty support they give in shopping with us'. His father, in retirement on his farm, had returned the favour, buying the district's first Eclipse reaping machines from Brittain Pash.

The wheelwright was one of the essential figures in rural industry. This photograph is believed to show Robert Punt's business at West Hanningfield, founded in the 1850s.

The Marconi Company's, and the world's, first wireless factory was established in Hall Street, Chelmsford, in 1898. This is its 70,000 square foot replacement, opened in June 1912 in New Street, on the site of the old sports and cricket ground, and still occupied by the firm today. Spalding must have taken this photograph soon afterwards, for it shows only one of the two 450-foot masts which became such a feature of the town's skyline, and which were reported in October 1912 to be 'rapidly rising'. In 1920, these masts carried the first true British broadcasts, and by 1931 there was 1 wireless licence for every 3 homes in the county.

Below are two views inside the factory, still impressive for the scale and degree of organization of the manufacturing process. The machine shop remained a male preserve, but the condenser and mounting shop reveals the openings for female employment in the new electrical industries.

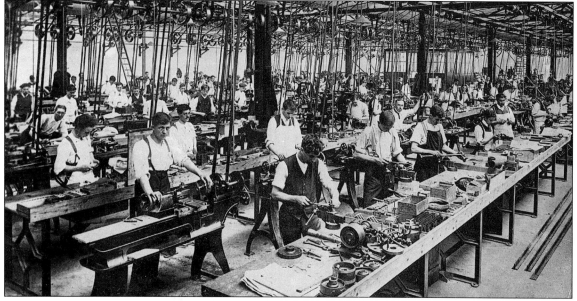

Gathering Speed

An anonymous waggoner – Fred junior
thought he came from Rettendon – poses in the
Spalding studio. The details of his clothing,
especially his smocked jacket, and the layout of
the studio, suggest a date in the 1860s (compare
the brewery workers on page 83). At that time,
William Harrod, the landlord of the Wheatsheaf
in Rettendon, ran a twice-weekly carrier's
waggon to Chelmsford.

A coach, either privately hired or belonging to
the local carrier, makes a stop at about the turn
of the century beside the River Wid at Writtle.
On the left is the mill house which used to serve
Writtle windmill, blown down in 1879. To the
right is Writtle watermill, rebuilt in brick at
about the same time, which continued in use
until 1957, but is now a burnt-out ruin.

A light gig of the early 1900s, outside the Red Cow Temperance Hotel in the Broomfield Road, Chelmsford. The hotel (formerly the 'Red Cow British Workman') was established in 1877, the year when a potent mixture of evangelical religion and hostility to alcohol gave rise to the movement known as Gospel Temperance. The name 'Red Cow' was perhaps an attempt to reclaim the biblical animal (Numbers xix.2) celebrated for its purity, but also used as a conventional inn sign. On the other hand, the wall plate behind the gig is advertising Bovril . . .

More elegant locomotion was provided by this Double Victoria, a form of carriage highly fashionable from the 1870s, after it was patronized by the Prince of Wales. Its low-slung body and lack of doors made it particularly accommodating for elaborate feminine fashions: these probably date from about the turn of the century.

The Eastern Counties Railway – incorporated into the Great Eastern in 1862 – reached Chelmsford in 1843. This is the town's second station, built in 1856 to replace a wooden building some 200 yards to the north. In 1892, probably close to the date of this photograph, an annual season ticket to Liverpool Street cost £22, or £17 8s. second class. The line also had something of a reputation for punctuality.

A Great Eastern goods train steams into Billericay, the line between Shenfield and Southend having been opened in 1889 in one of the last major extensions of the local network. The express passenger service to London, operated through Shenfield from 1911, helped to stimulate the modern development of Billericay, but the 'Official Guide to the Great Eastern Railway' in 1892 still described it as 'a tiny market town of some fifteen hundred inhabitants, picturesquely perched on the summit of a lofty hill which commands charming views'.

Hoffmann's ball-bearing factory in Chelmsford, nationalized in 1917, was greatly expanded in the last months of the First World War to cope with demand from the Ministry of Munitions. The contractor, Henry Martin of Northampton, brought in this small steam engine to haul materials for the works.

91

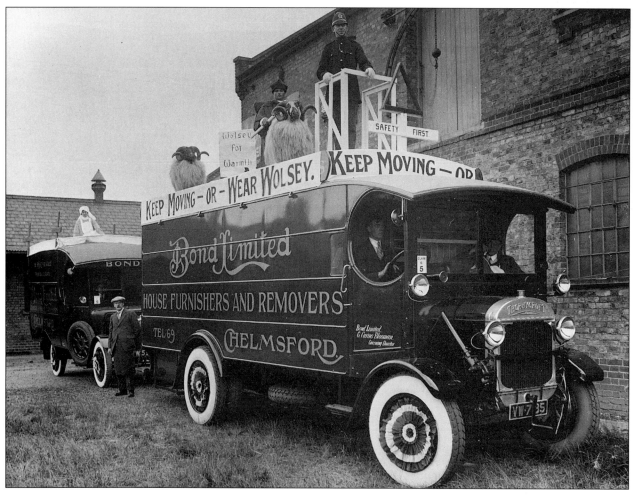

Fred Spalding took a great interest in the van-dressing competitions of Chelmsford's inter-war carnivals, and took great pains over his own entries. His rival here is J. G. Bond Ltd., general drapers, and forerunners of Debenhams store. They registered this Thornycroft pantechnicon in November 1928, and entered it in the carnival of 1929.

The Pollard's Garage stand at the 66th Essex Show, staged in Hylands Park in May 1928. Their 'exhibits specially suitable for agriculturalists' included milk delivery vans, cattle trucks, and 'a car readily convertible from a 4-seater pleasure car to a combined passenger and goods-carrying vehicle'. This point of economy was perhaps especially welcome to farmers, under such financial pressure that the machinery makers actually boycotted the show in protest. More than £700 was raised for show funds by a local collection committee run, inevitably, by Fred Spalding: 'as an Essex man, he had been pleased to do what he could to help the Essex Show'.

Three types of transport occupy the Broomfield Road, Chelmsford, in about 1905. On the left, a hand-cart carrying the wide baskets of a delivery-man; in the centre, a light horse-drawn carriage; and on the right, a steel-tyred Mann steam lorry of 1904, owned by Choat & Son, builders and contractors. This empty, tree-lined street would not remain so for long. Fred Spalding later wrote on the mount of this photograph: 'note the beautiful trees all gone, now shops'. As a young man, he had looked out at the trees from 17 Broomfield Road, where he lived with his wife and infant children.

The 250,000th British-built Ford makes a promotional stop in May 1925 at the inappositely named Austin's Garage, on the corner of Rainsford Road and Coval Lane, Chelmsford (the site is now covered by offices). Built at Trafford Park, Manchester, the car was on a 3600-mile tour of Great Britain, and also stopped at West Ham, Southend and Colchester. Spalding, who was mayor at the time, stands here in a light hat, under the word 'Supplies'. Distinctive corporate lettering was one aspect of Ford's vigorous marketing effort, emphasizing reliability and value for money (a Ford tourer in 1925 cost £125). The opening of the huge Dagenham works in 1931 gave further force to their slogan, 'You Support British Industry When You Buy Your Ford'.

An unexpectedly poetic shot of a Pollard's mechanic polishing up a mud-guard.

One of Pollard's Garage's customers was the Essex County Constabulary, which decided in 1933 to provide cars for detectives working out of Brentwood, Chelmsford, Grays and Romford. Using trains and buses was said to involve 'a considerable loss of time and efficiency'. Here are the 4

Austin Sevens supplied, at a total cost of £750, outside the police headquarters in Springfield. Two years later, with an average of 25,000 miles on the clock, they were replaced by Ford Eights.

A charabanc full of excursionists stops at the King's Head, Great Baddow, between 1925 and 1929. High-bodied vehicles like this, with a door for every passenger, would shortly be replaced by lower-level coaches, such as those above right. It is interesting that the King's Head sign here has

'stuck' at Edward VII (d.1910): perhaps the English pub was already becoming a location for nostalgia. The sign has now regressed to Henry VIII.

The history of bus transport has a special place for Chelmsford, since the Clarkson Works, which had been making steam buses from 1903, became the headquarters of the National Steam Car Company. Operating in London from 1909, National buses worked locally from 1913; Eastern National appeared in 1930. Here is a view of Chelmsford bus station in Duke Street, taken shortly before its demolition and replacement by the spanking new station, below, opened in July 1931. Even this proved inadequate, and was rebuilt again in 1937, Fairfield House – visible in the background here – being demolished to allow expansion westwards. Once more, Spalding was consciously documenting a historical process. A letter of 1934 survives, in which he asks the station manager for information for his 'record of the various great changes in the shops and public buildings'.

In May 1932, Prince George (later Duke of Kent) flew into Chelmsford Aerodrome in his personal Gipsy Moth, in order to open the town's first bypass, between Widford – the location of the photograph above – and Springfield. Built partly with unemployed labour from the 'distressed areas', its main purpose was the wholly modern one of keeping traffic out of town. The Prince went on to visit Marconi's, Hoffmann's and Crompton's works, before standing at a Marconi microphone on the steps of Oaklands Park to open the County Fayre and Social Services Exhibition. His whole programme emphasized modernity and progress – proof, to quote his speech, of 'the ability and keenness for improvement and new ideas of the Borough of Chelmsford'. What Spalding felt we do not know: probably pride in the forward march of his native town; perhaps regret at the end of an era when a town's affairs could be concentrated into the few narrow streets at its centre. At all events it seems a suitable moment to leave him: the world of our eminent Victorian was truly passing on.